To M. C. S. and J. H. S.,
Under whose rooftree these translations were made.

PLAYS

AUGUST STRINDBERG

PLAYS

THE FATHER
COUNTESS JULIE
THE OUTLAW
THE STRONGER

TRANSLATED BY
EDITH AND WARNER OLAND

BIBLIOBAZAAR

PLAYS

CONTENTS

THE FATHER 23
  A Tragedy in III Acts.

COUNTESS JULIE 78
  A Tragedy in I Act.

THE OUTLAW 123
  A play in I Act.

THE STRONGER 154
  An Episode in I Scene.

BIOGRAPHICAL NOTE

"I tell you, you must have chaos in you, if you would give birth to a dancing star."—Nietzsche.

In Stockholm, living almost as a recluse, August Strindberg is dreaming life away. The dancing stars, sprung from the chaos of his being, shine with an ever-increasing refulgence from the high-arched dome of dramatic literature, but he no longer adds to their number. The constellation of the Lion of the North is complete.

At sixty-three, worn by the emotional intensity of a life, into which has been crowded the stress and storm of a universe, he sits at his desk, every day transcribing to his diary a record of those mystical forces which he says regulate his life.

Before him lies a crucifix, Hardly as a symbol of sectarian faith, for Strindberg is a Swedenborgian, but a fitting accompaniment, nevertheless, to a state of mind which he expresses in saying "One gets more and more humble the longer one lives, and in the shadow of death many things look different." A softer light beams from those blue eyes, which, under that tossing crown of tawny hair flung high from a speaking forehead, in times past flashed defiance at every opposition. For him the fierce, unyielding, never-ceasing, ever-pressing strife of mind and unrest of life is passing, an eddy in the tide has borne him into quieter waters, and if the hum of the world reaches his solitude, it no longer rouses him to headlong action.

Secure in his position as the foremost man of letters Sweden has produced in modern times, the last representative of that distinguished group of Scandinavian writers which included Ibsen, Bjornson and Brandes, with a Continental reputation surpassing that of any one of them, Strindberg well may be entitled to dream of the past.

One day when in the evolution of the drama Strindberg's technique shall have served its purpose and like Ibsen's, be forced to give way before the advance of younger artists, when his most radical views shall have become the commonplaces of pseudo-culture, the scientific psychologist will take the man in hand and, from the minute record of his life, emotions, thoughts, fancies, speculations and nightmares, which he has embodied in autobiographical novels and that most remarkable perhaps of all his creations, abysmal in its pessimism, "The Inferno," will be drawn a true conception of the man.

That the individual will prove quite as interesting a study as his literary work, even the briefest outline of Strindberg's life will suggest.

The lack of harmony in his soul that has permeated his life and work with theses and antitheses Strindberg tries to explain through heredity, a by no means satisfying or complete solution for the motivation of his frequently unusual conduct and exceptional temperamental qualities, which the abnormal psychologist is in the habit of associating with that not inconsiderable group of cases in which the emotional and temperamental characteristics of the opposite sex are dominant in the individual. His ancestry has been traced back to the sixteenth century, when his father's family was of the titled aristocracy, later, generation after generation, becoming churchmen, although Strindberg's father, Carl Oscar, undertook a commercial career. His mother, Ulrica Eleanora Norling, was the daughter of a poor tailor, whom Strindberg's father first met as a waitress in a hotel, and, falling in love with her, married, after she had borne him three children.

August, christened Johann August, the fourth child, was born at Stockholm, January 22, 1849, soon after his father had become a bankrupt. There was little light or cheer in the boy's home; the misfortune that overtook the family at the time of August's birth always hung over them like a dark cloud; the mother became nervous and worn from the twelve child-births she survived, the father serious and reserved. The children were brought up strictly and as August was no favorite, loneliness and hostility filled even his earliest years.

His first school days were spent among boys of the better class, who turned up their noses at his leather breeches and heavy boots. He was taken away from that school and sent where there was a lower class of boys, whose leader he soon became, but in his studies he was far from precocious, though not dull.

As he grew up the family fortunes bettered, and he attended a private school patronized by cultivated and wealthy people. Mixing so with both classes meant much in the development of the youth, and he began to realize that he belonged to both and neither, felt homeless, torn in his sympathies and antipathies, plebian and aristocratic at the same time. In his thirteenth year, his mother died, a loss for which his father was apparently soon consoled, as in less than a year he married his housekeeper. This was another blow to the boy, for he disliked the woman, and there was soon war between them.

At fifteen he fell in love with it woman of thirty of very religious character, and its this was a period of fervent belief with the youth himself, she became an influence in his life for Home time, but one day a young comrade asked him to luncheon at a cafe, and for the first time Strindberg partook of schnaps and ale with a hearty meal. This little luncheon was the event which broke up the melancholy introspection of his youth and stirred him to activity.

He went to Upsala University for one term and then left, partly on account of the lack of funds for books, and partly because the slow, pedantic methods of learning were distasteful to his restless, active nature. He then became a school teacher; next interested in medical science, which he studied energetically, until the realities of suffering drove him from it. About this time, the same time, by the way, that Ibsen's "The League of Youth" was being hissed down at Christiana, the creative artist in Strindberg began to stir, and after six months more of turmoil of soul, he turned to the stage as a possible solution, making his debut at the Dramatiska Theatre in 1869 in Bjornson's "Mary Stuart," in the part of a lord with one line to speak. After two months of no advancement he found courage to ask to be heard in one of the classical roles he had been studying.

The director, tired from a long rehearsal, reluctantly consented to listen to him, likewise, the bored company of actors. Strindberg went on "to do or die," and was soon shouting like a revivalist, and made such it bad impression that he was advised to go to the dramatic school to study. He went home disgusted and heartsick, and, determined to take his life, swallowed an opium pill which he had long been keeping for that purpose.

However, it was not sufficiently powerful, and, a friend coming to see him, he was persuaded to go out, and together they drowned his chagrin in an evening at it cafe.

The day after was a memorable one, for it was Strindberg's birthday as a dramatist. He was lying on a sofa at home, his body still hot from the shame of his defeat—and wine, trying to figure out how he could persuade his stepmother to effect a reconciliation between him and his father. He saw the scenes played as clearly as though on a stage, and with his brain working at high pressure, in two hours had the scheme for two acts of a comedy worked out. In four days it was finished—Strindberg's first play! It was refused production, but he was complimented, and felt that his honor was saved.

The fever of writing took possession of him and within two months he had finished two comedies, and a tragedy in verse called "Hermione," which was later produced. Giving so much promise as a dramatist he was persuaded to leave the stage and, unwilling of spirit, returned to Upsala in the spring of 1870, as he was advised that he would never he recognized as a writer unless he had secured is university degree. The means with which to continue his studies were derived from the two hundred crowns left him by his mother, which he now forced his father to allow him to use. Despite this, however, his fortunes often ran to the lowest ebb.

One day Strindberg announced that he had a one act play called "In Rome" to read to the "Runa" (Song) Club, a group of six students whom he had gotten together, and which was devoted exclusively to the reading of the poetry of its members. The play, based upon an incident in the life of Thorvaldsen, was received enthusiastically by the "Runa," and the rest of the night was spent in high talk of Strindberg's future over a champagne supper in his honor given by one of the well-to-do members. These days of homage and appreciation from this student group Strindberg cherishes as the happiest time in his life, but notwithstanding their worshipful attitude, he himself was full of doubts and misgivings about his abilities.

One of these friends sent the manuscript of "In Rome" to the Dramatiska Theatre at Stockholm, where it was accepted and produced anonymously in August of the same year, 1870. Strindberg was present at the premiere and although it was well received, to him it was all a fine occasion—except the play! He was ashamed of his self-confession in it and fled before the final curtain. He soon finished another play, "The Outlaw," which is included in the present volume. In this drama, which retains a high place among his plays, Strindberg shows for the first time his lion's claw and in it began to speak with his own voice. It was accepted by the Court Theatre at Stockholm for production during the next autumn, that of 1871.

At the close of the summer, after a violent quarrel with his father, he returned to the University in the hope of finding help from his comrades. Arrived at Upsala, with just one crown, he found that many of his old and more prosperous friends were no longer there. Times were harder than ever.

But at last a gleam of hope came with the news that "The Outlaw" was actually to be produced. And his wildest dreams were then realized, for, despite the unappreciative attitude of the critics toward this splendid Viking piece, the King, Carl XV, after seeing the play, commanded Strindberg to appear before him. Strindberg regarded the summons as the perpetration of a practical joke, and only obeyed it after making sure by telegraph that it was not a hoax.

Strindberg tells of the kindly old king standing with a big pipe in his hand as the young author strode between chamberlains and other court dignitaries into the royal presence.

The king, a grandson of Napoleon's marshal Bernadotte, and as a Frenchman on the throne of Sweden, diplomatic enough to desire at least the appearance of being more Swedish than the Swedes, spoke of the pleasure the ancient Viking spirit of "The Outlaw" had given him, and, after talking genially for some time, said, "You are the son of Strindberg, the steamship agent, I believe and so, of course, are not in need."

"Quite the reverse," Strindberg replied, explaining that his father no longer gave him the meager help in his university course, which he had formerly done.

"How much can you get along on per annum until you graduate?" asked the king.

Strindberg was unable to say in a moment. "I'm rather short of coin myself," said the king quite frankly, "but do you think you could manage on eight hundred riksdaler a year?" Strindberg was overwhelmed by such munificence, and the interview was concluded by his introduction to the court treasurer, from whom he received his first quarter's allowance of two hundred crowns.

Full of thankfulness for this unexpected turn of fate, the young dramatist returned to Upsala. For once he appeared satisfied with his lot, and took up his studies with more earnestness than ever. The year 1871 closed brilliantly for the young writer, for in addition to the kingly favor be received honorable mention from the Swedish Academy for his Greek drama "Hermione." The following year, 1872, life at the university again began to pall on his restless mind, and he took to painting.

Then followed a serious disagreement with one of the professors, so that when he received word from the court treasurer that it was uncertain whether his stipend could be continued on account of the death of the king, he decided to leave the University for good. At a farewell banquet in his honor, he expressed his appreciation of all he had received from his student friends, saying, "A personality does not develop from itself, but out of each soul it comes in contact with, it sucks a drop, just as the bee gathers its honey from a million flowers giving it forth eventually as its own."

Strindberg went to Stockholm to become a literateur and, if possible, a creative artist. He gleaned a living from newspaper work for a few months, but in the summer went to a fishing village on a remote island in Bothnia Bay where, in his twenty-third year, he wrote his great historical drama, "Master Olof." Breaking away from traditions and making flesh and blood creations instead of historical skeletons in this play, it was refused by all the managers of the theatres, who assured Strindberg that the public would not tolerate any such unfamiliar methods. Strindberg protested, and defended and tried to elucidate his realistic handling of the almost sacred historical personages, but in vain, for "Master Olof" was not produced until seven years later, when it was put on at the Swedish Theatre at Stockholm in 1880, the year Ibsen was writing "Ghosts" at Sorrento.

In 1874, after a year or two of unsuccessful effort to make a living in various employments, he became assistant at the Court library, which was indeed a haven of refuge, a position providing both leisure for study and an assured income. Finding in the library some Chinese parchments which had not been catalogued; he plunged into the study of that language. A treatise which he wrote on the subject won him medals from various learned societies at home, as well as recognition from the French Institute. This success induced the many other treatises that followed, for which he received a variety of decorations, and along with the honors nearly brought upon himself "a salubrious idiocy," to use his own phrase.

Then something happened that stirred the old higher voice in him,—he fell in love. He had been invited through a woman friend to go to the home of Baron Wrangel, where his name as an author was esteemed. He refused the invitation, but the next day, walking in the city streets with this same woman friend, they encountered the Baroness Wrangel to whom Strindberg was introduced. The Baroness asked him once more to come. He promised to do so, and they separated. As Strindberg's friend went into a shop, he turned to look down the street; noting the beautiful lines of the disappearing figure of the Baroness, noting, too, a stray lock of her golden hair, that had escaped from her veil, and played against the white ruching at her throat. He gazed after her long, in fact, until she disappeared in the crowded street. From that moment he was not a free man. The friendship which followed resulted in the divorce of the Baroness from her husband and her marriage to Strindberg, December 30, 1877, when he was twenty-eight years old. At last Strindberg had someone to love, to take care of, to worship. This experience of happiness, so strange to him, revived the creative impulse.

The following year, 1878, "Master Olof" was finally accepted for publication, and won immediate praise and appreciation. This, to his mind, belated success, roused in Strindberg a smoldering resentment, which lack of confidence and authority of position had heretofore caused him to repress. He broke out with a burning satire, in novel form, called "The Red Room," the motto of which he made Voltaire's words "Rien n'est si desagreable que s'etre pendu obscurement."

Hardly more than mention can be made of the important work of this dramatist, poet, novelist, historian, scientist and philosopher. In 1888 he left Sweden, as the atmosphere there had become too disagreeable for him through controversy after controversy in which lie became involved. He joined a group of painters and writers of all nationalities in it little village in France. There he wrote "La France," setting forth the relations between France and Sweden in olden times. This was published in Paris and the French government, tendered him the decoration of the legion of honor which, however, he refused very politely, explaining that he never wore a frock coat! The episode ends amusingly with the publisher, a Swede, receiving the decoration instead. In 1884 the first volume of his famous short stories, called "Marriages" appeared. It was aimed at the cult that had sprung up from Ibsen's "A Doll's House," which was threatening the peace of all households. A few days after the publication of "Marriages" the first edition was literally swallowed up. As the book dealt frankly with the physical facts of sex relations, it was confiscated by the Swedish government a month after its publication, and Strindberg was obliged to go to Stockholm to defend his cause in the courts, which he won, and in another month "Marriages" was again on the market.

The next year, 1885, his "Real Utopias" was written in Switzerland, an attack, in the form of four short stories, on over-civilization, which won him much applause in Germany. He went to Italy as a special correspondent for the "Daily News" of Stockholm.

In 1886 the much anticipated second volume of "Marriages" appeared. These were the short stories, satisfying to the simplest as well as to the most discriminating minds, that attracted Nietzsche's attention to Strindberg. A correspondence sprung up between the two men, referring to which in a letter to Peter Gast, Nietzsche said, "Strindberg has written to me, and for the first time I sense an answering note of universality." The mutual admiration and intellectual sympathies of these two conspicuous creative geniuses has led a number of critics, including Edmund Gosse, into the error of attributing to Nietzsche a dominating influence over Strindberg. It should be remembered, however, the "Countess Julie" and "The Father," which are cited its the most obvious examples of that supposed influence, were completed before Strindberg's acquaintance with Nietzsche's philosophy, and that among others, the late John Davidson, is also charged with having drawn largely from Nietzsche. The fact is, that, during the last quarter of the nineteenth century, the most original thinkers of many countries were quite independently, though less clearly, evolving the same philosophic principals that the master mind of Nietzsche was radiating in the almost blinding flashes of his genius.

Then came the period during which Strindberg attained the highest peaks of his work, the years 1886-90, with his autobiography, "The Servant Woman's Son," the tragedies, "The Father," and "Countess Julie," the comedies, "Comrades," and "The Stronger," and the tragi-comedies, "The Creditors" and "Simoon." Of these, "The Father" and "Countess Julie" soon made Strindberg's name known and honored throughout Europe, except in his home country.

In "The Father" perhaps his biggest vision is felt. It was published in French soon after it appeared in Sweden, with an introduction by Zola in which he says, "To be brief, you have written a mighty and capitvating work. It is one of the few dramas that have had the power to stir me to the depths."

Of his choice of theme in "Countess Julie," Strindberg says: "When I took this motive from life, as it was related to me a few years ago, it made a strong impression on me. I found it suitable for tragedy, and it still makes a sorrowful impression on me to see an individual to whom happiness has been allotted go under, much more, to see a line become extinct." And in defence of his realism he has said further in his preface to "Countess Julie": "The theatre has for a long time seemed to me the Biblia pauperum in the fine arts, a bible with pictures for those who can neither read nor write, and the dramatist is the revivalist, and the revivalist dishes tap the ideas of the day in popular form, so popular that the middle class, of whom the bulk of theatre-goers is comprised, can without burdening their brains understand what it is all about. The theatre therefore has always been a grammar school for the young, the half-educated, and women, who still possess the primitive power of being able to delude themselves and of allowing themselves to be deluded, that is to say, receive illusions and accept suggestions from the dramatist. *** Some people have accused my tragedy, 'The Father' of being too sad, as though one desired a merry tragedy. People call authoritatively for the 'Joy of Life' and theatrical managers call for farces, as though the Joy of Life lay in being foolish, and in describing people who each and every one are suffering from St. Vitus' dance or idiocy. I find the joy of life in the powerful, terrible struggles of life; and the capability of experiencing something, of learning something, is a pleasure to me. And therefore I have chosen an unusual but instructive subject; in other words, an exception, but a great exception, that will strengthen the rules which offend the apostle of the commonplace. What will further create antipathy in some, is the fact that my plan of action is not simple, and that there is not one view alone to be taken of it. An event in life—and that is rather a new discovery—is usually occasioned by a series of more or less deep-seated motifs, but the spectator generally chooses that one which his power of judgment finds simplest to grasp, or that his gift of judgment considers the most honorable. For example, someone commits suicide: 'Bad business!' says the citizen; 'Unhappy love!' says the woman; 'Sickness!' says the sick man; 'Disappointed hopes?' the bankrupt. But it may be that none of these reasons is the real one, and that the dead man hid the real one by pretending another that would throw the most favorable light on his memory. *** In the following drama ('Julie') I have not sought to do anything new, because that cannot be done, but only to modernize the form according to the requirements I have considered present-day people require."

Following the mighty output, of those years, in 1891 Strindberg went out: to the islands where he had lived years before, and led a hermit's life. Many of his romantic plays were written there, and much of his time was spent at painting.

In 1892 he was divorced from his wife.

After a few months Strindberg went to Berlin, where he was received with all honors by literary Germany. Richard Dehmel, one of their foremost minstrels, celebrated the event by a poem called "An Immortal,—To Germany's Guest." In the shop windows his picture hung alongside that of Bismarck, and at the theatres his plays were being produced. About this time he heard of the commotion that "Countess Julie" had created in Paris, where it had been produced by Antoine. During these victorious times Strindberg met a young Austrian writer, Frida Uhl, to whom he was married in April 1898. Although the literary giant of the hour, he was nevertheless in very straightened pecuniary circumstances, which led to his allowing the publication of "A Fool's Confession," written in French, and later, with out his permission or knowledge, issued in German and Swedish, which entangled him in a lawsuit, as the subject matter contained much of his marital miseries. Interest in chemistry had long been stirring in Strindberg's mind; it now began to deepen. About this time also he passed through that religious crisis which swept artistic Europe, awakened nearly a century after his death by that Swedenborgian poet and artist, William Blake. To this period belongs "To Damascus," a play of deepest soul probing, which was not finished however until 1904.

Going to Paris in the fall of 1894, to pursue chemical research most seriously, he ran into his own success at the theatres there. "The Creditors" had been produced and Strindberg was induced to undertake the direction of "The Father" at the Theatre de l'Oeuvre, where it was a tremendous success. A Norwegian correspondent was forced to send word home that with "The Father" Strindberg had overreached Ibsen in Paris, because what it had never been possible to do with an Ibsen play, have a run in Paris, they were now doing with Strindberg. At the same time the Theatre des Ecaliers put on "The Link," the Odean produced "The Secret of the Guild," and the Chat Noir "The Kings of Heaven," and translations of his novels were running in French periodicals. But Strindberg turned his back on all this success and shut himself up in his laboratory to delve into chemistry. This he did with such earnestness that with his discovery of Swedenborg his experimentations and speculations reduced him to a condition of mind that unfitted him for any kind of companionship, so that when his wife left him to go to their child who was ill and far away, he welcomed the complete freedom. Strindberg says of their parting at the railway station that although they smiled and waved to each other as they called out "Auf wiedersehen" they both knew that they were saying good bye forever, which proved to be true, as they were divorced a year later. In 1896 he returned to Sweden so broken in health through his tremendous wrestling with the riddle of life that he went into the sanitorium of his friend, Dr. Aliasson at Wstad. After two months he was sufficiently restored to go to Austria, at the invitation of his divorced wife's family, to see his child. Then back to Sweden, to Lund, a university town, where he lived solely to absorb Swedenborg. By May of that year he was able to go to work on "The Inferno," that record of a soul's nightmare, which in all probability will remain unique in the history of literature. Then came the writing of the great historical dramas, then the realistically symbolic plays of Swedenborgian spirit, of which "Easter" is representative, and the most popular.

When "Easter" was produced in Stockholm a young Norwegian, Harriet Bosse, played Eleanora, the psychic, and in 1901 this young actress became Strindberg's wife. This third marriage ended in divorce three years later. In 1906, the actor manager, August Folk, produced "Countess Julie" in Stockholm, seventeen years after it had been written. To Strindberg's amazement, it won such tremendous attention that the other theatres became deserted. In consequence of this success an intimate theatre was founded for the production of none but Strindberg's plays.

How he is estimated today in his own country may be judged by the following extract from an article which appeared in a recent issue of the leading periodical of Stockholm:

> "For over thirty years he has dissected us from every point of view; during that time his name has always been conspicuous in every book-shop window and his books gradually push out the others from our shelves; every night his plays are produced at the theatres; every conversation turns on him, and his is the name the pigmies quarrel over daily; the cry is heard that he has become hysterical, sentimental, out of his mind, but the next one knows, he is robustness itself, and enduring beyond belief, despite great need, enmity, sorrow. One hour one is angry over some extravagance which he has allowed himself, the next captivated by one of his plays, stirred, melted, strengthened and uplifted by his sublime genius."

THE FATHER

CHARACTERS
    A CAPTAIN OF CAVALRY
    LAURA, his wife
    BERTHA, their daughter
    DOCTOR OSTERMARK
    THE PASTOR
    THE NURSE
    NOEJD
    AN ORDERLY

ACT I.

[The sitting room at the Captain's. There is a door a little to the right at the back. In the middle of the room, a large, round table strewn with newspapers and magazines. To right a leather-covered sofa and table. In the right-hand corner a private door. At left there is a door leading to the inner room and a desk with a clock on it. Gamebags, guns and other arms hang on the walls. Army coats hang near door at back. On the large table stands a lighted lamp.]

CAPTAIN [rings, an orderly comes in.]

ORDERLY. Yes, Captain.

CAPTAIN. Is Noejd out there?

ORDERLY. He is waiting for orders in the kitchen.

CAPTAIN. In the kitchen again, is he? Send him in at once.

ORDERLY. Yes, Captain. [Goes.]

PASTOR. What's the matter now?

CAPTAIN. Oh the rascal has been cutting up with the servant-girl again; he's certainly a bad lot.

PASTOR. Why, Noejd got into the same trouble year before last, didn't he?

CAPTAIN. Yes, you remember? Won't you be good enough to give him a friendly talking to and perhaps you can make some impression on him. I've sworn at him and flogged him, too, but it hasn't had the least effect.

PASTOR. And so you want me to preach to him? What effect do you suppose the word of God will have on a rough trooper?

CAPTAIN. Well, it certainly has no effect on me.

PASTOR. I know that well enough.

CAPTAIN. Try it on him, anyway.

[Noejd comes in.]

CAPTAIN. What have you been up to now, Noejd?

NOEJD. God save you, Captain, but I couldn't talk about it with the Pastor here.

PASTOR. Don't be afraid of me, my boy.

CAPTAIN. You had better confess or you know what will happen.

NOEJD. Well, you see it was like this; we were at a dance at Gabriel's, and then—then Ludwig said—

CAPTAIN. What has Ludwig got to do with it? Stick to the truth.

NOEJD. Yes, and Emma said "Let's go into the barn—"

CAPTAIN.—Oh, so it was Emma who led you astray, was it?

NOEJD. Well, not far from it. You know that unless the girl is willing nothing ever happens.

CAPTAIN. Never mind all that: Are you the father of the child or not?

NOEJD. Who knows?

CAPTAIN. What's that? Don't you know?

NOEJD. Why no—that is, you can never be sure.

CAPTAIN. Weren't you the only one?

NOEJD. Yes, that time, but you can't be sure for all that.

CAPTAIN. Are you trying to put the blame on Ludwig? Is that what you are up to?

NOEJD. Well, you see it isn't easy to know who is to blame.

CAPTAIN. Yes, but you told Emma you would marry her.

NOEJD. Oh, a fellow's always got to say that—

CAPTAIN [to Pastor.] This is terrible, isn't it?

PASTOR. It's the old story over again. See here, Noejd, you surely ought to know whether you are the father or not?

NOEJD. Well, of course I was mixed up with the girl—but you know yourself, Pastor, that it needn't amount to anything for all that.

PASTOR. Look here, my lad, we are talking about you now. Surely you won't leave the girl alone with the child. I suppose we can't compel you to marry her, but you should provide for the child— that you shall do!

NOEJD. Well, then, so must Ludwig, too.

CAPTAIN. Then the case must go to the courts. I cannot ferret out the truth of all this, nor is it to my liking. So now be off.

PASTOR. One moment, Noejd. H'm—don't you think it dishonorable to leave a girl destitute like that with her child? Don't you think so? Don't you see that such conduct——h'm—h'm——

NOEJD. Yes, if I only knew for sure that I was father of the child, but you can't be sure of that, Pastor, and I don't see much fun slaving all your life for another man's child. Surely you, Pastor, and the Captain can understand for yourselves.

CAPTAIN. Be off.

NOEJD. God save you, Captain. [Goes.]

CAPTAIN. But keep out of the kitchen, you rascal! [To Pastor.] Now, why didn't you get after him?

PASTOR. What do you mean?

CAPTAIN. Why, you only sat and mumbled something or other.

PASTOR. To tell the truth I really don't know what to say. It is a pity about the girl, yes, and a pity about the lad, too. For think if he were not the father. The girl can nurse the child for four months at the orphanage, and then it will be permanently provided for, but it will be different for him. The girl can get a good place afterwards in some respectable family, but the lad's future may be ruined if he is dismissed from the regiment.

CAPTAIN. Upon my soul I should like to be in the magistrate's shoes and judge this case. The lad is probably not innocent, one can't be sure, but we do know that the girl is guilty, if there is any guilt in the matter.

PASTOR. Well, well, I judge no one. But what were we talking about when this stupid business interrupted us? It was about Bertha and her confirmation, wasn't it?

CAPTAIN. Yes, but it was certainly not in particular about her confirmation but about her whole welfare. This house is full of women who all want to have their say about my child. My mother-in-law wants to make a Spiritualist of her. Laura wants her to be an artist; the governess wants her to be a Methodist, old Margret a Baptist, and the servant-girls want her to join the Salvation Army! It won't do to try to make a soul in patches like that. I, who have the chief right to try to form her character, am constantly opposed in my efforts. And that's why I have decided to send her away from home.

PASTOR. You have too many women trying to run this house.

CAPTAIN. You're right! It's like going into a cage full of tigers, and if I didn't hold a red-hot iron under their noses they would tear me to pieces any moment. And you laugh, you rascal! Wasn't it enough that I married your sister, without your palming off your old stepmother on me?

PASTOR. But, good heavens, one can't have stepmothers in one's own house!

CAPTAIN. No, you think it is better to have mothers-in-law in some one else's house!

PASTOR. Oh well, we all have some burden in life.

CAPTAIN. But mine is certainly too heavy. I have my old nurse into the bargain, who treats me as if I ought still to wear a bib. She is a good old soul, to be sure, and she must not be dragged into such talk.

PASTOR. You must keep a tight rein on the women folks. You let them run things too much.

CAPTAIN. Now will you please inform me how I'm to keep order among the women folk?

PASTOR. Laura was brought up with a firm hand, but although she is my own sister, I must admit she *was* pretty troublesome.

CAPTAIN. Laura certainly has her faults, but with her it isn't so serious.

PASTOR. Oh, speak out—I know her.

CAPTAIN. She was brought up with romantic ideas, and it has been hard for her to find herself, but she is my wife—

PASTOR And because she is your wife she is the best of wives? No, my dear fellow, it is she who really wears on you most.

CAPTAIN. Well, anyway, the whole house is topsy-turvy. Laura won't let Bertha leave her, and I can't allow her to remain in this bedlam.

PASTOR. Oh, so Laura won't? Well, then, I'm afraid you are in for trouble. When she was a child if she set her mind on anything she used to play dead dog till she got it, and then likely as not she would give it back, explaining that it wasn't the thing she wanted, but having her own way.

CAPTAIN. So she was like that even then? H'm—she really gets into such a passion sometimes that I am anxious about her and afraid she is ill.

PASTOR. But what do you want to do with Bertha that is so unpardonable? Can't you compromise?

CAPTAIN. You mustn't think I want to make a prodigy of her or an image of myself. I don't want to be it procurer for my daughter and educate her exclusively for matrimony, for then if she were left unmarried she might have bitter days. On the other hand, I don't want to influence her toward a career that requires a long course of training which would be entirely thrown away if she should marry.

PASTOR. What do you want, then?

CAPTAIN. I want her to be it teacher. If she remains unmarried she will be able to support herself, and at any rate she wouldn't be any worse off than the poor schoolmasters who have to share their salaries with a family. If she marries she can use her knowledge in the education of her children. Am I right?

PASTOR. Quite right. But, on the other hand, hasn't she shown such talent for painting that it would be a great pity to crush it?

CAPTAIN. No! I have shown her sketches to an eminent painter, and he says they are only the kind of thing that can be learned at schools. But then a young fop came here in the summer who, of course, understands the matter much better, and he declared that she had colossal genius, and so that settled it to Laura's satisfaction.

PASTOR. Was he quite taken with Bertha?

CAPTAIN. That goes without saying.

PASTOR. Then God help you, old man, for in that case I see no hope. This is pretty bad—and, of course, Laura has her supporters—in there?

CAPTAIN. Yes, you may be sure of that; the whole house is already up in arms, and, between ourselves, it is not exactly a noble conflict that is being waged from that quarter.

PASTOR. Don't you think I know that?

CAPTAIN. You do?

PASTOR. I do.

CAPTAIN. But the worst of it is, it strikes me that Bertha's future is being decided from spiteful motives. They hint that men better be careful, because women can do this or that now-a-days. All day long, incessantly, it is a conflict between man and woman. Are you going? No, stay for supper. I have no special inducements to offer, but do stay. You know I am expecting the new doctor. Have you seen him?

PASTOR. I caught a glimpse of him as I came along. He looked pleasant, and reliable.

CAPTAIN. That's good. Do you think it possible he may become my ally?

PASTOR. Who can tell? It depends on how much he has been among women.

CAPTAIN. But won't you really stay?

PASTOR. No thanks, my dear fellow; I promised to be home for supper, and the wife gets uneasy if I am late.

CAPTAIN. Uneasy? Angry, you mean. Well, as you will. Let me help you with your coat.

PASTOR. It's certainly pretty cold tonight. Thanks. You must take care of your health, Adolf, you seem rather nervous.

CAPTAIN. Nervous?

PASTOR. Yes, you are not, really very well.

CAPTAIN. Has Laura put that into your head? She has treated me for the last twenty years as if I were at the point of death.

PASTOR. Laura? No, but you make me uneasy about you. Take care of yourself—that's my advice! Good-bye, old man; but didn't you want to talk about the confirmation?

CAPTAIN. Not at all! I assure you that matter will have to take its course in the ordinary way at the cost of the clerical conscience for I am neither a believer nor a martyr.

PASTOR. Good-bye. Love to Laura. [Goes.]

[The Captain opens his desk and seats himself at it.
Takes up account books.]

CAPTAIN [Figuring.] Thirty-four—nine, forty-three—seven, eight, fifty-six—

LAURA [Coming in from inner room.] Will you be kind enough—

CAPTAIN. Just a moment! Sixty-six—seventy-one, eighty-four, eighty-nine, ninety-two, a hundred. What is it?

LAURA. Am I disturbing you?

CAPTAIN. Not at all. Housekeeping money, I suppose?

LAURA. Yes, housekeeping money.

CAPTAIN. Put the accounts down there and I will go over them.

LAURA. The accounts?

CAPTAIN. Yes.

LAURA. Am I to keep accounts now?

CAPTAIN. Of course you are to keep accounts. Our affairs are in a precarious condition, and in case of a liquidation, accounts are necessary, or one is liable to punishment for being careless.

LAURA. It's not my fault that our affairs are in a precarious condition.

CAPTAIN. That is exactly what the accounts will decide.

LAURA. It's not my fault that our tenant doesn't pay.

CAPTAIN. Who recommended this tenant so warmly? You! Why did you recommend a—good-for-nothing, we'll call him?

LAURA. But why did you rent to this good-for-nothing?

CAPTAIN. Because I was not allowed to eat in peace, nor sleep in peace, nor work in peace, till you women got that man here. You wanted him so that your brother might be rid of him, your mother wanted him because I didn't want him, the governess wanted him because he reads his Bible, and old Margret because she had known his grandmother from childhood. That's why he was taken, and if he hadn't been taken, I'd be in a madhouse by now or lying in my grave. However, here is the housekeeping money and your pin money. You may give me the accounts later.

LAURA [Curtesies.] Thanks so much. Do you too keep an account of what you spend besides the housekeeping money?

CAPTAIN. That doesn't concern you.

LAURA. No, that's true—just as little as my child's education concerns me. Have the gentlemen come to a decision after this evening's conference?

CAPTAIN. I had already come to a decision, and therefore it only remained for me to talk it over with the one friend I and the family have in common. Bertha is to go to boarding school in town, and starts in a fortnight.

LAURA. To which boarding school, if I may venture to ask?

CAPTAIN. Professor Saefberg's.

LAURA. That free thinker!

CAPTAIN. According to the law, children are to be brought up in their father's faith.

LAURA. And the mother has no voice in the matter?

CAPTAIN. None whatever. She has sold her birthright by a legal transaction, and forfeited her rights in return for the man's responsibility of caring for her and her children.

LAURA. That is to say she has no rights concerning her child.

CAPTAIN. No, none at all. When once one has sold one's goods, one cannot have them back and still keep the money.

LAURA. But if both father and mother should agree?

CAPTAIN. Do you think that could ever happen? I want her to live in town, you want her to stay at home. The arithmetical result would be that she remain at the railway station midway between train and home. This is a knot that cannot be untied, you see.

LAURA. Then it must be broken. What did Noejd want here?

CAPTAIN. That is an official secret.

LAURA. Which the whole kitchen knows!

CAPTAIN. Good, then you must know it.

LAURA. I do know it.

CAPTAIN. And have your judgment ready-made?

LAURA. My judgment is the judgment of the law.

CAPTAIN. But it is not written in the law who the child's father is.

LAURA. No, but one usually knows that.

CAPTAIN. Wise minds claim that one can never know.

LAURA. That's strange. Can't one ever know who the father of a child is?

CAPTAIN. No; so they claim.

LAURA. How extraordinary! How can the father have such control over the children then?

CAPTAIN. He has control only when he has assumed the responsibilities of the child, or has had them forced upon him. But in wedlock, of course, there is no doubt about the fatherhood.

LAURA. There are no doubts then?

CAPTAIN. Well, I should hope not.

LAURA. But if the wife has been unfaithful?

CAPTAIN. That's another matter. Was there anything else you wanted to say?

LAURA. Nothing.

CAPTAIN. Then I shall go up to my room, and perhaps you will be kind enough to let me know when the doctor arrives. [Closes desk and rises]

LAURA. Certainly.

[Captain goes through the primate door right.]

CAPTAIN. As soon as he comes. For I don't want to seem rude to him, you understand. [Goes.]

LAURA. I understand. [Looks at the money she holds in her hands.]

MOTHER-IN-LAW'S VOICE [Within.] Laura!

LAURA. Yes.

MOTHER-IN-LAW'S VOICE. Is my tea ready?

LAURA [In doorway to inner room]. In just a moment.

[Laura goes toward hall door at back as the orderly opens it.]

ORDERLY. Doctor Ostermark.

DOCTOR. Madam!

LAURA [Advances and offers her hand]. Welcome, Doctor—you are heartily welcome. The Captain is out, but he will be back soon.

DOCTOR. I hope you will excuse my coming so late, but I have already been called upon to pay some professional visits.

LAURA. Sit down, won't you?

DOCTOR. Thank you.

LAURA. Yes, there is a great deal of illness in the neighborhood just now, but I hope it will agree with you here. For us country people living in such isolation it is of great value to find a doctor who is interested in his patients, and I hear so many nice things of you, Doctor, that I hope the pleasantest relations will exist between us.

DOCTOR. You are indeed kind, and I hope for your sake my visits to you will not often be caused by necessity. Your family is, I believe, as a rule in good health—

LAURA. Fortunately we have bear spared acute illnesses, but still things are not altogether as they should be.

DOCTOR. Indeed?

LAURA. Heaven knows, things are not as might be wished.

DOCTOR. Really, you alarm me.

LAURA. There are some circumstances in a family which through honor and conscience one is forced to conceal from the whole world—

DOCTOR. Excepting the doctor.

LAURA. Exactly. It is, therefore, my painful duty to tell you the whole truth immediately.

DOCTOR. Shouldn't we postpone this conference until I have had the honor of being introduced to the Captain?

LAURA. No! You must hear me before seeing him.

DOCTOR. It relates to him then?

LAURA. Yes, to him, my poor, dear husband.

DOCTOR. You alarm me, indeed, and believe me, I sympathize with your misfortune.

LAURA [Taking out handkerchief]. My husband's mind is affected. Now you know all, and may judge for yourself when you see him.

DOCTOR. What do you say? I have read the Captain's excellent treatises on mineralogy with admiration, and have found that they display a clear and powerful intellect.

LAURA. Really? How happy I should be if we should all prove to be mistaken.

DOCTOR. But of course it is possible that his mind might be affected in other directions.

LAURA. That is just what we fear, too. You see he has sometimes the most extraordinary ideas which, of course, one might expect in a learned man, if they did not have a disastrous effect on the welfare of his whole family. For instance, one of his whims is buying all kinds of things.

DOCTOR. That is serious; but what does he buy?

LAURA. Whole boxes of books that he never reads.

DOCTOR. There is nothing strange about a scholar's buying books.

LAURA. You don't believe what I am saying?

DOCTOR. Well, Madam, I am convinced that you believe what you are saying.

LAURA. Tell me, is it reasonable to think that one can see what is happening on another planet by looking through a microscope?

DOCTOR. Does he say he can do that?

LAURA. Yes, that's what he says.

DOCTOR. Through a microscope?

LAURA. Through a microscope, yes.

DOCTOR. This is serious, if it is so.

LAURA. If it is so! Then you have no faith in me, Doctor, and here I sit confiding the family secret to—

DOCTOR. Indeed, Madam, I am honored by your confidence, but as a physician I must investigate and observe before giving an opinion. Has the Captain ever shown any symptoms of indecision or instability of will?

LAURA. Has he! We have been married twenty years, and he has never yet made a decision without changing his mind afterward.

DOCTOR. Is he obstinate?

LAURA. He always insists on having his own way, but once he has got it he drops the whole matter and asks me to decide.

DOCTOR. This is serious, and demands close observation. The will, you see, is the mainspring of the mind, and if it is affected the whole mind goes to pieces.

LAURA. God knows how I have taught myself to humor his wishes through all these long years of trial. Oh, if you knew what a life I have endured with him—if you only knew.

DOCTOR. Your misfortune touches me deeply, and I promise you to see what can be done. I pity you with all my heart, and I beg you to trust me completely. But after what I have heard I must ask you to avoid suggesting any ideas that might make a deep impression on the patient, for in a weak brain they develop rapidly and quickly turn to monomania or fixed ideas.

LAURA. You mean to avoid arousing suspicions?

DOCTOR. Exactly. One can make the insane believe anything, just because they are receptive to everything.

LAURA. Indeed? Then I understand. Yes—yes. [A bell rings within.] Excuse me, my mother wishes to speak to me. One moment—Ah, here is Adolf.

[Captain comes in through private door.]

CAPTAIN. Oh, here already, Doctor? You are very welcome.

DOCTOR. Captain! It is a very great pleasure to me to make the acquaintance of so celebrated a man of science.

CAPTAIN. Oh, I beg of you. The duties of service do not allow me to make any very profound investigations, but I believe I am now really on the track of a discovery.

DOCTOR. Indeed?

CAPTAIN. You see, I have submitted meteoric stones to spectrum analysis, with the result that I have found carbon, that, is to say, a clear trace of organic life. What do you say to that?

DOCTOR. Can you see that with it microscope?

CAPTAIN. Lord, no—with the spectroscope.

DOCTOR. The spectroscope! Pardon. Then you will soon be able to tell us what is happening on Jupiter.

CAPTAIN. Not what is happening, but what has happened. If only the confounded booksellers in Paris would send me the books; but I believe all the booksellers in the universe have conspired against me. Think of it, for the last two months not a single one has ever answered my communications, neither letters nor abusive telegrams. I shall go mad over it, and I can't imagine what's the matter.

DOCTOR. Oh, I suppose it's the usual carelessness; you mustn't let it vex you so.

CAPTAIN. But the devil of it is I shall not get my treatise done in time, and I know they are working along the same lines in Berlin. But we shouldn't be talking about this—but about you. If you care to live here we have rooms for you in the wing, or perhaps you would rather live in the old quarters?

DOCTOR. Just as you like.

CAPTAIN. No, as you like. Which is it to be?

DOCTOR. You must decide that, Captain.

CAPTAIN. No, it's not for me to decide. You must say which you prefer. I have no preference in the matter, none at all.

DOCTOR. Oh, but I really cannot decide.

CAPTAIN. For heaven's sake, Doctor, say which you prefer. I have no choice in the matter, no opinion, no wishes. Haven't you got character enough to know what you want? Answer me, or I shall be provoked.

DOCTOR. Well, if it rests with me, I prefer to live here.

CAPTAIN. Thank you—forgive me, Doctor, but nothing annoys me so touch as to see people undecided about anything. [Nurse comes in.] Oh, there you are, Margret. Do you happen to know whether the rooms in the wing are in order for the Doctor?

NURSE. Yes, sir, they are.

CAPTAIN. Very well. Then I won't detain you, Doctor; you must be tired. Good bye, and welcome once more. I shall see you tomorrow, I hope.

DOCTOR. Good evening, Captain.

CAPTAIN. I daresay that my wife explained conditions here to you a little, so that you have some idea how the land lies?

DOCTOR. Yes, your excellent wife has given me a few hints about this and that, such as were necessary to a stranger. Good evening, Captain.

CAPTAIN [To Nurse]. What do you want, you old dear? What is it?

NURSE. Now, little Master Adolf, just listen—

CAPTAIN. Yes, Margret, you are the only one I can listen to without having spasms.

NURSE. Now, listen, Mr. Adolf. Don't you think you should go half-way and come to an agreement with Mistress in this fuss over the child? Just think of a mother—

CAPTAIN. Think of a father, Margret.

NURSE. There, there, there. A father has something besides his child, but a mother has nothing but her child.

CAPTAIN. Just so, you old dear. She has only one burden, but I have three, and I have her burden too. Don't you think that I should hold a better position in the world than that of a poor soldier if I had not had her and her child?

NURSE. Well, that isn't what I wanted to talk about.

CAPTAIN. I can well believe that, for you wanted to make it appear that I am in the wrong.

NURSE. Don't you believe, Mr. Adolf, that I wish you well?

CAPTAIN. Yes, dear friend, I do believe it; but you don't know what is for my good. You see it isn't enough for me to have given the child life, I want to give her my soul, too.

NURSE. Such things I don't understand. But I do think that you ought to be able to agree.

CAPTAIN. You are not my friend, Margret.

NURSE. I? Oh, Lord, what are you saying, Mr. Adolf? Do you think I can forget that you were my child when you were little?

CAPTAIN. Well, you dear, have I forgotten it? You have been like a mother to me, and always have stood by me when I had everybody against me, but now, when I really need you, you desert me and go over to the enemy.

NURSE. The enemy!

CAPTAIN, Yes, the enemy! You know well enough how things are in this house! You have seen everything from the beginning.

NURSE. Indeed I have seen! But, God knows, why two people should torment the life out of each other; two people who are otherwise so good and wish all others well. Mistress is never like that to me or to others—

CAPTAIN. Only to me, I know it. But let me tell you, Margret, if you desert me now, you will do wrong. For now they have begun to weave a plot against me, and that doctor is not my friend.

NURSE. Oh, Mr. Adolf, you believe evil about everybody. But you see it's because you haven't the true faith; that's just what it is.

CAPTAIN. Yes, you and the Baptists have found the only true faith. You are indeed lucky!

NURSE. Anyway, I'm not unhappy like you, Mr. Adolf. Humble your heart and you will see that God will make you happy in your love for your neighbor.

CAPTAIN. It's a strange thing that you no sooner speak of God and love than your voice becomes hard and your eyes fill with hate. No, Margret, surely you have not the true faith.

NURSE. Yes, go on being proud and hard in your learning, but it won't amount to much when it comes to the test.

CAPTAIN. How mightily you talk, humble heart. I know very well that knowledge is of no use to you women.

NURSE. You ought to be ashamed of yourself. But in spite of everything old Margret cares most for her great big boy, and he will come back to the fold when it's stormy weather.

CAPTAIN. Margret! Forgive me, but believe me when I say that there is no one here who wishes me well but you. Help me, for I feel that something is going to happen here. What it is, I don't know, but something evil is on the way. [Scream from within.] What's that? Who's that screaming?

[Berths enters from inner room.]

BERTHA. Father! Father! Help me; save me.

CAPTAIN. My dear child, what is it? Speak!

BERTHA. Help me. She wants to hurt me.

CAPTAIN. Who wants to hurt you? Tell me! Speak!

BERTHA. Grandmother! But it's my fault for I deceived her.

CAPTAIN. Tell me more.

BERTHA. Yes, but you mustn't say anything about it. Promise me you won't.

CAPTAIN. Tell me what it is then.

[Nurse goes.]

BERTHA. In the evening she generally turns down the lamp and then she makes me sit at a table holding a pen over a piece of paper. And then she says that the spirits are to write.

CAPTAIN. What's all this—and you have never told me about it?

BERTHA. Forgive me, but I dared not, for Grandmother says the spirits take revenge if one talks about them. And then the pen writes, but I don't know whether I'm doing it or not. Sometimes it goes well, but sometimes it won't go at all, and when I am tired nothing comes, but she wants it to come just the same. And tonight I thought I was writing beautifully, but then grandmother said it was all from Stagnelius, and that I had deceived her, and then she got terribly angry.

CAPTAIN. Do you believe that there are spirits?

BERTHA. I don't know.

CAPTAIN. But I know that there are none.

BERTHA. But Grandmother says that you don't understand, Father, and that you do much worse things—you who can see to other planets.

CAPTAIN. Does she say that! Does she say that? What else does she say?

BERTHA. She says that you can't work witchery.

CAPTAIN. I never said that I could. You know what meteoric stones are,—stones that fall from other heavenly bodies. I can examine them and learn whether they contain the same elements as our world. That is all I can tell.

BERTHA. But Grandmother says that there are things that she can see which you cannot see.

CAPTAIN. Then she lies.

BERTHA. Grandmother doesn't tell lies.

CAPTAIN. Why doesn't she?

BERTHA. Then Mother tells lies too.

CAPTAIN. H'm!

BERTHA. And if you say that Mother lies, I can never believe in you again.

CAPTAIN. I have not said so; and so you must believe in me when I tell you that it is for your future good that you should leave home. Will you? Will you go to town and learn something useful?

BERTHA. Oh, yes, I should love to go to town, away from here, anywhere. If I can only see you sometimes—often. Oh, it is so gloomy and awful in there all the time, like a winter night, but when you come home Father, it is like a morning in spring when they take off the double windows.

CAPTAIN. My beloved child! My dear child!

BERTHA. But, Father, you'll be good to Mother, won't you? She cries so often.

CAPTAIN. H'm—then you want to go to town?

BERTHA. Yes, yes.

CAPTAIN. But if Mother doesn't want you to go?

BERTHA. But she must let me.

CAPTAIN. But if she won't?

BERTHA. Well, then, I don't know what will happen. But she must! She must!

CAPTAIN. Will you ask her?

BERTHA. You must ask her very nicely; she wouldn't pay any attention to my asking.

CAPTAIN. H'm! Now if you wish it, and I wish it, and she doesn't wish it, what shall we do then?

BERTHA. Oh, then it will all be in a tangle again! Why can't you both—

[Laura comes in.]

LAURA. Oh, so Bertha is here. Then perhaps we may have her own opinion as the question of her future has to be decided.

CAPTAIN. The child can hardly have any well-grounded opinion about what a young girl's life is likely to be, while we, on the contrary, can more easily estimate what it may be, as we have seen so many young girls grow up.

LAURA. But as we are of different opinions Bertha must be the one to decide.

CAPTAIN. No, I let no one usurp my rights, neither women nor children. Bertha, leave us.

[Bertha goes out.]

LAURA. You were afraid of hearing her opinion, because you thought it would be to my advantage.

CAPTAIN. I know that she wishes to go away from home, but I know also that you possess the power of changing her mind to suit your pleasure.

LAURA. Oh, am I really so powerful?

CAPTAIN. Yes, you have a fiendish power of getting your own way; but so has anyone who does not scruple about, the way it is accomplished. How did you get Doctor Norling away, for instance, and how did you get this new doctor here?

LAURA. Yes, how did I manage that?

CAPTAIN. You insulted the other one so much that he left, and made your brother recommend this fellow.

LAURA. Well, that was quite simple and legitimate. Is Bertha to leave home now?

CAPTAIN. Yes, she is to start in a fortnight.

LAURA. That is your decision?

CAPTAIN. Yes.

LAURA. Then I must try to prevent it.

CAPTAIN. You cannot.

LAURA. Can't I? Do you really think I would trust my daughter to wicked people to have her taught that everything her mother has implanted in her child is mere foolishness? Why, afterward, she would despise me all the rest of her life!

CAPTAIN. Do you think that a father should allow ignorant and conceited women to teach his daughter that he is a charlatan?

LAURA. It means less to the father.

CAPTAIN. Why so?

LAURA. Because the mother is closer to the child, as it has been discovered that no one can tell for a certainty who the father of a child is.

CAPTAIN. How does that apply to this case?

LAURA. You do not know whether you are Bertha's father or not.

CAPTAIN. I do not know?

LAURA. No; what no one knows, you surely cannot know.

CAPTAIN. Are you joking?

LAURA. No; I am only making use of your own teaching. For that matter, how do you know that I have not been unfaithful to you?

CAPTAIN. I believe you capable of almost anything, but not that, nor that you would talk about it if it were true.

LAURA. Suppose that I was prepared to bear anything, even to being despised and driven out, everything for the sake of being able to keep and control my child, and that I am truthful now when I declare that Bertha is my child, but not yours. Suppose—

CAPTAIN. Stop now!

LAURA. Just suppose this. In that case your power would be at an end.

CAPTAIN. When you had proved that I was not the father.

LAURA. That would not be difficult! Would you like me to do so?

CAPTAIN. Stop!

LAURA. Of course I should only need to declare the name of the real father, give all details of place and time. For instance—when was Bertha born? In the third year of our marriage.

CAPTAIN. Stop now, or else—

LAURA. Or else, what? Shall we stop now? Think carefully about all you do and decide, and whatever you do, don't make yourself ridiculous.

CAPTAIN. I consider all this most lamentable.

LAURA. Which makes you all the more ridiculous.

CAPTAIN. And you?

LAURA. Oh, we women are really too clever.

CAPTAIN. That's why one cannot contend with you.

LAURA. Then why provoke contests with a superior enemy?

CAPTAIN. Superior?

LAURA. Yes, it's queer, but I have never looked at a man without knowing myself to be his superior.

CAPTAIN. Then you shall be made to see your superior for once, so that you shall never forget it.

LAURA. That will be interesting.

NURSE [comes in]. Supper is served. Will you come in?

LAURA. Very well.

> [Captain lingers; sits down with a magazine in an arm chair near table.]

LAURA. Aren't you coming in to supper?

CAPTAIN. No, thanks. I don't want anything.

LAURA. What, are you annoyed?

CAPTAIN. No, but I am not hungry.

LAURA. Come, or they will ask unnecessary questions—be good now. You won't? Stay there then. [Goes.]

NURSE. Mr. Adolf! What is this all about?

CAPTAIN. I don't know what it is. Can you explain to me why you women treat an old man as if he were a child?

NURSE. I don't understand it, but it must be because all you men, great and small, are women's children, every man of you.

CAPTAIN. But no women are born of men. Yes, but I am Bertha's father. Tell me, Margret, don't you believe it? Don't you?

NURSE. Lord, how silly you are. Of course you are your own child's father. Come and eat now, and don't sit there and sulk. There, there, come now.

CAPTAIN. Get out, woman. To hell with the hags. [Goes to private door.] Svaerd, Svaerd!

> [Orderly comes in.]

ORDERLY. Yes, Captain.

CAPTAIN. Hitch into the covered sleigh at once.

NURSE. Captain, listen to me.

CAPTAIN. Out, woman! At once!

[Orderly goes.]

NURSE. Good Lord, what's going to happen now.

[Captain puts on his cap and coat and prepares to go out.]

CAPTAIN. Don't expect me home before midnight. [Goes.]

NURSE. Lord preserve us, whatever will be the end of this!

ACT II.

[The same scene as in previous act. A lighted lamp is on the table; it is night. The Doctor and Laura are discovered at rise of curtain.]

DOCTOR. From what I gathered during my conversation with him the case is not fully proved to me. In the first place you made a mistake in saying that he had arrived at these astonishing results about other heavenly bodies by means of a microscope. Now that I have learned that it was a spectroscope, he is not only cleared of any suspicion of insanity, but has rendered a great service to science.

LAURA. Yes, but I never said that.

DOCTOR. Madam, I made careful notes of our conversation, and I remember that I asked about this very point because I thought I had misunderstood you. One must be very careful in making such accusations when a certificate in lunacy is in question.

LAURA. A certificate in lunacy?

DOCTOR. Yes, you must surely know that an insane person loses both civil and family rights.

LAURA. No, I did not know that.

DOCTOR. There was another matter that seemed to me suspicious. He spoke of his communications to his booksellers not being answered. Permit me to ask if you, through motives of mistaken kindness, have intercepted them?

LAURA. Yes, I have. It was my duty to guard the interests of the family, and I could not let him ruin us all without some intervention.

DOCTOR. Pardon me, but I think you cannot have considered the consequences of such an act. If he discovers your secret interference in his affairs, he will have grounds for suspicions, and they will grow like an avalanche. And besides, in doing this you have thwarted his will and irritated him still more. You must have felt yourself how the mind rebels when one's deepest desires are thwarted and one's will is crossed.

LAURA. Haven't I felt that!

DOCTOR. Think, then, what he must have gone through.

LAURA [Rising]. It is midnight and he hasn't come home. Now we may fear the worst.

DOCTOR. But tell me what actually happened this evening after I left. I must know everything.

LAURA. He raved in the wildest way and had the strangest ideas. For instance, that he is not the father of his child.

DOCTOR. That is strange. How did such an idea come into his head?

LAURA. I really can't imagine, unless it was because he had to question one of the men about supporting a child, and when I tried to defend the girl, he grew excited and said no one could tell who was the father of a child. God knows I did everything to calm him, but now I believe there is no help for him. [Cries.]

DOCTOR. But this cannot go on. Something must be done here without, of course, arousing his suspicions. Tell me, has the Captain ever had such delusions before?

LAURA. Six years ago things were in the same state, and then he, himself, confessed in his own letter to the doctor that he feared for his reason.

DOCTOR. Yes, yes, yes, this is a story that has deep roots and the sanctity of the family life—and so on—of course I cannot ask about everything, but must limit myself to appearances. What is done can't be undone, more's the pity, yet the remedy should be based upon all the past.—Where do you think he is now?

LAURA. I have no idea, he has such wild streaks.

DOCTOR. Would you like to have me stay until he returns? To avoid suspicion, I could say that I had come to see your mother who is not well.

LAURA. Yes, that will do very nicely. Don't leave us, Doctor; if you only knew how troubled I am! But wouldn't it be better to tell him outright what you think of his condition.

DOCTOR. We never do that unless the patient mentions the subject himself, and very seldom even then. It depends entirely on the case. But we mustn't sit here; perhaps I had better go into the next room; it will look more natural.

LAURA. Yes, that will be better, and Margret can sit here. She always waits up when he is out, and she is the only one who has any power over him. [Goes to the door left] Margret, Margret!

NURSE. Yes, Ma'am. Has the master come home?

LAURA. No; but you are to sit here and wait for him, and when he does come you are to say my mother is ill and that's why the doctor is here.

NURSE. Yes, yes. I'll see that everything is all right.

LAURA [Opens the door to inner rooms]. Will you come in here, Doctor?

DOCTOR. Thank you.

[Nurse seats herself at the table and takes up a hymn book
and spectacles and reads.]

NURSE. Ah, yes, ah yes!

[Reads half aloud]

Ah woe is me, how sad a thing
Is life within this vale of tears,
Death's angel triumphs like a king,
    And calls aloud to all the spheres—
            Vanity, all is vanity.
    Yes, yes! Yes, yes!

[Reads again]

All that on earth hath life and breath
To earth must fall before his spear,
And sorrow, saved alone from death,
Inscribes above the mighty bier.
            Vanity, all is vanity.
Yes, Yes.

BERTHA [Comes in with a coffee-pot and some embroidery.
She speaks in a low voice]. Margret, may I sit with you? It is so
frightfully lonely up there.

NURSE. For goodness sake, are you still up, Bertha?

BERTHA. You see I want to finish Father's Christmas present.
And here's something that you'll like.

NURSE. But bless my soul, this won't do. You must be up in the
morning, and it's after midnight now.

BERTHA. What does it matter? I don't dare sit up there alone. I
believe the spirits are at work.

NURSE. You see, just what I've said. Mark my words, this house
was not built on a lucky spot. What did you hear?

BERTHA. Think of it, I heard some one singing up in the attic!

NURSE. In the attic? At this hour?

BERTHA. Yes, it was such it sorrowful, melancholy song! I never heard anything like it. It sounded as if it came from the store-room, where the cradle stands, you know, to the left——

NURSE. Dear me, Dear me! And such a fearful night. It seems as if the chimneys would blow down. "Ah, what is then this earthly life, But grief, afiction and great strife? E'en when fairest it has seemed, Nought but pain it can be deemed." Ah, dear child, may God give us a good Christmas!

BERTHA. Margret, is it true that Father is ill?

NURSE. Yes, I'm afraid he is.

BERTHA. Then we can't keep Christmas eve? But how can he be up and around if he is ill?

NURSE. You see, my child, the kind of illness he has doesn't keep him from being up. Hush, there's some one out in the hall. Go to bed now and take the coffee pot away or the master will be angry.

BERTHA [Going out with tray]. Good night, Margret.

NURSE. Good night, my child. God bless you.

[Captain comes in, takes off his overcoat.]

CAPTAIN. Are you still up? Go to bed.

NURSE. I was only waiting till—

[Captain lights a candle, opens his desk, sits down at it and takes letters and newspapers out of his pocket.]

NURSE. Mr. Adolf.

CAPTAIN. What do you want?

NURSE. Old mistress is ill and the doctor is here.

CAPTAIN. Is it anything dangerous?

NURSE. No, I don't think so. Just a cold.

CAPTAIN [Gets up]. Margret, who was the father of your child?

NURSE. Oh, I've told you many and many a time; it was that scamp Johansson.

CAPTAIN. Are you sure that it was he?

NURSE. How childish you are; of course I'm sure when he was the only one.

CAPTAIN. Yes, but was he sure that he was the only one? No, he could not be, but you could be sure of it. There is a difference, you see.

NURSE. Well, I can't see any difference.

CAPTAIN. No, you cannot see it, but the difference exists, nevertheless. [Turns over the pages of a photograph album which is on the table.] Do you think Bertha looks like me?

NURSE. Of course! Why, you are as like as two peas.

CAPTAIN. Did Johansson confess that he was the father?

NURSE. He was forced to!

CAPTAIN. How terrible! Here is the Doctor. [Doctor comes in.] Good evening, Doctor. How is my mother-in-law?

DOCTOR. Oh, it's nothing serious; merely a slight sprain of the left ankle.

CAPTAIN. I thought Margret said it was a cold. There seem to be different opinions about the same case. Go to bed, Margret.

[Nurse goes. A pause.]

CAPTAIN. Sit down, Doctor.

DOCTOR [Sits]. Thanks.

CAPTAIN. Is it true that you obtain striped foals if you cross a zebra and a mare?

DOCTOR [Astonished]. Perfectly true.

CAPTAIN. Is it true that the foals continue to be striped if the breed is continued with a stallion?

DOCTOR. Yes, that is true, too.

CAPTAIN. That is to say, under certain conditions a stallion can be sire to striped foals or the opposite?

DOCTOR. Yes, so it seems.

CAPTAIN. Therefore an offspring's likeness to the father proves nothing?

DOCTOR. Well——

CAPTAIN. That is to say, paternity cannot be proven.

DOCTOR. H'm—well—

CAPTAIN. You are a widower, aren't you, and have had children?

DOCTOR. Ye-es.

CAPTAIN. Didn't you ever feel ridiculous as a. father? I know of nothing so ludicrous as to see a father leading his children by the hand around the streets, or to hear it father talk about his children. "My wife's children," he ought to say. Did you ever feel how false your position was? Weren't you ever afflicted with doubts, I won't say suspicions, for, as a gentleman, I assume that your wife was above suspicion.

DOCTOR. No, really, I never was; but, Captain, I believe Goethe says a man must take his children on good faith.

CAPTAIN. It's risky to take anything on good faith where a woman is concerned.

DOCTOR. Oh, there are so many kinds of women.

CAPTAIN. Modern investigations have pronounced that there is only one kind! Lately I have recalled two instances in my life that make me believe this. When I was young I was strong and, if I may boast, handsome. Once when I was making a trip on a steamer and sitting with a few friends in the saloon, the young stewardess came and flung herself down by me, burst into tears, and told us that her sweetheart was drowned. We sympathized with her, and I ordered some champagne. After the second glass I touched her foot; after the fourth her knee, and before morning I had consoled her.

DOCTOR. That was just a winter fly.

CAPTAIN. Now comes the second instance—and that was a real summer fly. I was at Lyskil. There was a young married woman stopping there with her children, but her husband was in town. She was religious, had extremely strict principles, preached morals to me, and was, I believe, entirely honorable. I lent her a book, two books, and when she was leaving, she returned them, strange to say! Three months later, in those very books I found her card with a declaration on it. It was innocent, as innocent its it declaration of love can be from a married woman to a strange man who never made any advances. Now comes the moral: Just don't have too much faith.

DOCTOR. Don't have too little faith either.

CAPTAIN. No, but just enough. But, you see, Doctor, that woman was so unconsciously dishonest that she talked to her husband about the fancy she had taken to me. That's what makes it dangerous, this very unconsciousness of their instinctive dishonesty. That is a mitigating circumstance, I admit, but it cannot nullify judgment, only soften it.

DOCTOR. Captain, your thoughts are taking a morbid turn, and you ought to control them.

CAPTAIN. You must not use the word morbid. Steam boilers, as you know, explode at it certain pressure, but the same pressure is not needed for all boiler explosions. You understand? However, you are here to watch me. If I were not a man I should have the right to make accusations or complaints, as they are so cleverly called, and perhaps I should be able to give you the whole diagnosis, and, what is more, the history of my disease. But unfortunately, I am a man, and there is nothing for me to do but, like a Roman, fold my arms across my breast and hold my breath till I die.

DOCTOR. Captain, if you are ill, it will not reflect upon your honor as a man to tell me all. In fact, I ought to hear the other side.

CAPTAIN. You have had enough in hearing the one, I imagine. Do you know when I heard Mrs. Alving eulogizing her dead husband, I thought to myself what a damned pity it was the fellow was dead. Do you suppose that he would have spoken if he had been alive? And do you suppose that if any of the dead husbands came back they would be believed? Good night, Doctor. You see that I am calm, and you can retire without fear.

DOCTOR. Good night, then, Captain. I'm afraid. I can be of no further use in this case.

CAPTAIN. Are we enemies?

DOCTOR. Far from it. But it is too bad we cannot be friends. Good night.

[Goes. The Captain follows the Doctor to the door at back and then goes to the door at left and opens it slightly.]

CAPTAIN. Come in, and we'll talk. I heard you out there listening. [Laura, embarrassed. Captain sits at desk.] It is late, but we must come to some decision. Sit down. [Pause.] I have been at the post office tonight to get my letters. From these it appears that you have been keeping back my mail, both coming and going. The consequence of which is that the loss of time has its good as destroyed the result I expected from my work.

LAURA. It was an act of kindness on my part, as you neglected the service for this other work.

CAPTAIN. It was hardly kindness, for you were quite sure that some day I should win more honor from that, than from the service; but you were particularly anxious that I should not win such honors, for fear your own insignificance would be emphasized by it. In consequence of all this I have intercepted letters addressed to you.

LAURA. That was a noble act.

CAPTAIN. You see, you have, as you might say, a high opinion of me. It appears from these letters that, for some time past you have been arraying my old friends against me by spreading reports about my mental condition. And you Dave succeeded in your efforts, for now not more than one person exists from the Colonel down to the cook, who believes that I am sane. Now these are the facts about my illness; my mind is sound, as you know, so that I can take care of my duties in the service as well its my responsibilities as a father; my feelings are more or less under my control, as my will has not been completely undermined; but you have gnawed and nibbled at it so that it will soon slip the cogs, and then the whole mechanism will slip and go to smash. I will not appeal to your feelings, for you have none; that is your strength; but I will appeal to your interests.

LAURA. Let me hear.

CAPTAIN. You have succeeded in arousing my suspicions to such an extent that my judgment is no longer clear, and my thoughts begin to wander. This is the approaching insanity that you are waiting for, which may come at any time now. So you are face to face with the question whether it is more to your interest that I should be sane or insane. Consider. If I go under I shall lose the service, and where will you be then? If I die, my life insurance will fall to you. But if I take my own life, you will get nothing. Consequently, it is to your interest that I should live out my life.

LAURA. Is this a trap?

CAPTAIN. To be sure. But it rests with you whether you will run around it or stick your head into it.

LAURA. You say that you will kill yourself! You won't do that!

CAPTAIN. Are you sure? Do you think a man can live when he has nothing and no one to live for?

LAURA. You surrender, then?

CAPTAIN. No, I offer peace.

LAURA. The conditions?

CAPTAIN. That I may keep my reason. Free me from my suspicions and I give up the conflict.

LAURA. What suspicions?

CAPTAIN. About Bertha's origin.

LAURA. Are there any doubts about that?

CAPTAIN. Yes, I have doubts, and you have awakened them.

LAURA. I?

CAPTAIN. Yes, you have dropped them like henbane in my ears, and circumstances have strengthened them. Free me from the uncertainty; tell me outright that it is true and I will forgive you beforehand.

LAURA. How can I acknowledge a sin that I have not committed?

CAPTAIN. What does it matter when you know that I shall not divulge it? Do you think a man would go and spread his own shame broadcast?

LAURA. If I say it isn't true, you won't be convinced; but if I say it is, then you will be convinced. You seem to hope it is true!

CAPTAIN. Yes, strangely enough; it must be, because the first supposition can't be proved; the latter can be.

LAURA. Have you tiny ground for your suspicions?

CAPTAIN. Yes, and no.

LAURA. I believe you want to prove me guilty, so that you can get rid of me and then have absolute control over the child. But you won't catch me in any such snare.

CAPTAIN. Do you think that I would want to be responsible for another man's child, if I were convinced of your guilt?

LAURA. No, I'm sure you wouldn't, and that's what makes me know you lied just now when you said that you would forgive me beforehand.

CAPTAIN. [Rises]. Laura, save me and my reason. You don't seem to understand what I say. If the child is not mine I have no control over her and don't want to have any, and that is precisely what you do want, isn't it? But perhaps you want even more—to have power over the child, but still have me to support you.

LAURA. Power, yes! What has this whole life and death struggle been for but power?

CAPTAIN. To me it has meant more. I do not believe in a hereafter; the child was my future life. That was my conception of immortality, and perhaps the only one that has any analogy in reality. If you take that away from me, you cut off my life.

LAURA. Why didn't we separate in time?

CAPTAIN. Because the child bound us together; but the link became a chain. And how did it happen; how? I have never thought about this, but now memories rise up accusingly, condemningly perhaps. We had been married two years, and had no children; you know why. I fell ill and lay at the point of death. During a conscious interval of the fever I heard voices out in the drawing-room. It was you and the lawyer talking about the fortune that I still possessed. He explained that you could inherit nothing because we had no children, and he asked you if you were expecting to become a mother. I did not hear your reply. I recovered and we had a child. Who is its father?

LAURA. You.

CAPTAIN. No, I am not. Here is a buried crime that begins to stench, and what a hellish crime! You women have been compassionate enough to free the black slaves, but you have kept the white ones. I have worked and slaved for you, your child, your mother, your servants; I have sacrificed promotion and career; I have endured torture, flaggellation, sleeplessness, worry for your sake, until my hair has grown gray; and all that you might enjoy a life without care, and when you grew old, enjoy life over again in your child. I have borne everything without complaint, because I thought myself the father of your child. This is the commonest kind of theft, the most brutal slavery. I have had seventeen years of penal servitude and have been innocent. What can you give me in return for that?

LAURA. Now you are quite mad.

CAPTAIN. That is your hope!—And I see how you have labored to conceal your crime. I sympathized with you because I did not understand your grief. I have often lulled your evil conscience to rest when I thought I was driving away morbid thoughts. I have heard you cry out in your sleep and not wanted to listen. I remember now night before last—Bertha's birthday—it was between two and three in the morning, and I was sitting up reading; you shrieked, "Don't, don't!" as if someone were strangling you; I knocked on the wall—I didn't want to hear any more. I have had my suspicions for a long time but I did not dare to hear them confirmed. All this I have suffered for you. What will you do for me?

LAURA. What can I do? I will swear by God and all I hold sacred that you are Bertha's father.

CAPTAIN. What use is that when you have often said that a mother can and ought to commit any crime for her child? I implore you as a wounded man begs for a death blow, to tell me all. Don't you see I'm as helpless as a child? Don't you hear me complaining as to a mother? Won't you forget that I am a man, that I am a soldier who can tame men and beasts with a word? Like a sick man I only ask for compassion. I lay down the tokens of my power and implore you to have mercy on my life.

[Laura approaches him and lays her hand on his brow.]

LAURA. What! You are crying, man!

CAPTAIN. Yes, I am crying although I am a man. But has not a man eyes! Has not a man hands, limbs, senses, thoughts, passions? Is he not fed with the wine food, hurt by the same weapons, warmed and cooled by the same summer and winter as a woman? If you prick us do we not bleed? If you tickle us do we not laugh? And if you poison us, do we not die? Why shouldn't a man complain, a soldier weep? Because it is unmanly? Why is it unmanly?

LAURA. Weep then, my child, as if you were with your mother once more. Do you remember when I first came into your life, I was like a second mother? Your great strong body needed nerves; you were a giant child that had either come too early into the world, or perhaps was not wanted at all.

CAPTAIN. Yes, that's how it was. My father's and my mother's will was against my coming into the world, and consequently I was born

59

without a will. I thought I was completing myself when you and I became one, and therefore you were allowed to rule, and I, the commander at the barracks and before the troops, became obedient to you, grew through you, looked up to you as to it more highly-gifted being, listened to you as if I had been your undeveloped child.

LAURA. Yes, that's the way it was, and therefore I loved you as my child. But you know, you must have seen, when the nature of your feelings changed and you appeared as my lover that I blushed, and your embraces were joy that was followed by a remorseful conscience as if my blood were ashamed. The mother became the mistress. Ugh!

CAPTAIN. I saw it, but I did not understand. I believed you despised me for my unmanliness, and I wanted to win you as a woman by being a man.

LAURA. Yes, but there was the mistake. The mother was your friend, you see, but the woman was your enemy, and love between the sexes is strife. Do not think that I gave myself; I did not give, but I took—what I wanted. But you had one advantage. I felt that, and I wanted you to feel it.

CAPTAIN. You always had the advantage. You could hypnotize me when I was wide awake, so that I neither saw nor heard, but merely obeyed; you could give me a raw potato and make me imagine it was a peach; you could force me to admire your foolish caprices as though they were strokes of genius. You could have influenced me to crime, yes, even to mean, paltry deeds. Because you lacked intelligence, instead of carrying out my ideas you acted on your own judgment. But when at last I awoke, I realized that my honor had been corrupted and I wanted to blot out the memory by a great deed, an achievement, a discovery, or an honorable suicide. I wanted to go to war, but was not permitted. It was then that I threw myself into science. And now when I was about to reach out my hand to gather in its fruits, you chop off my arm. Now I am dishonored and can live no longer, for a man cannot live without honor.

LAURA. But a woman?

CAPTAIN. Yes, for she has her children, which he has not. But, like the rest of mankind, we lived our lives unconscious as children, full of imagination, ideals, and illusions, and then we awoke; it was all over. But we awoke with our feet on the pillow, and he who waked us was himself a sleep-walker. When women grow old and cease to be women, they get beards on their chins; I wonder what men get when they grow old and cease to be men. Those who crowed were no longer cocks but capons, and the pullets answered their call, so that when we thought the sun was about to rise we found ourselves in the bright moon light amid ruins, just as in the good old times. It had only been a little morning slumber with wild dreams, and there was no awakening.

LAURA. Do you know, you should have been a poet!

CAPTAIN. Who knows.

LAURA. Now I am sleepy, so if you have any more fantastic visions keep them till to-morrow.

CAPTAIN. First, a word more about realities. Do you hate me?

LAURA. Yes, sometimes, when you are a man.

CAPTAIN. This is like race hatred. If it is true that we are descended from monkeys, at least it must be from two separate species. We are certainly not like one another, are we?

LAURA. What do you mean to say by all this?

CAPTAIN. I feel that one of us must go under in this struggle.

LAURA. Which?

CAPTAIN. The weaker, of course.

LAURA. And the stronger will be in the right?

CAPTAIN. Always, since he has the power.

LAURA. Then I am in the right.

CAPTAIN. Have you the power already then?

LAURA. Yes, and a legal power with which I shall put you under the control of a guardian.

CAPTAIN. Under a guardian?

LAURA. And then I shall educate my child without listening to your fantastic notions.

CAPTAIN. And who will pay for the education when I am no longer here?

LAURA. Your pension will pay for it.

CAPTAIN [Threateningly]. How can you have me put under a guardian?

LAURA [Takes out a letter]. With this letter of which an attested copy is in the hands of the board of lunacy.

CAPTAIN. What letter?

LAURA [Moving backward toward the door left]. Yours! Your declaration to the doctor that you are insane. [The Captain stares at her in silence.] Now you have fulfilled your function as an unfortunately necessary father and breadwinner, you are not needed any longer and you must go. You must go, since you have realized that my intellect is as strong as my will, and since you will not stay and acknowledge it.

[The Captain goes to the table, seizes the lighted lamp and hurls it at Laura, who disappears backward through the door.]

CURTAIN DROP.

ACT III.

[Same Scene. Another lamp on the table. The private door is barricaded with a chair.]

LAURA [to Nurse]. Did he give you the keys?

NURSE. Give them to me, no! God help me, but I took them from the master's clothes that Noejd had out to brush.

LAURA. Oh, Noejd is on duty today?

NURSE. Yes, Noejd.

LAURA. Give me the keys.

NURSE. Yes, but this seems like downright stealing. Do you hear him walking up there, Ma'am? Back and forth, back and forth.

LAURA. Is the door well barred?

NURSE. Oh, yes, it's barred well enough!

LAURA. Control your feelings, Margret. We must be calm if we are to be saved. [Knock.] Who is it?

NURSE [Opens door to hall]. It is Noejd.

LAURA. Let him come in.

NOEJD [Comes in]. A message from the Colonel.

LAURA. Give it to me [Reads] Ah!—Noejd, have you taken all the cartridges out of the guns and pouches?

NOEJD. Yes, Ma'am.

LAURA. Good, wait outside while I answer the Colonel's letter. [Noejd goes. Laura writes.]

NURSE. Listen. What in the world is he doing up there now?

LAURA. Be quiet while I write.

[The sound of sawing is heard.]

NURSE [Half to herself]. Oh, God have mercy on us all! Where will this end!

LAURA. Here, give this to Noejd. And my mother must not know anything about all this. Do you hear?

[Nurse goes out, Laura opens drawers in desk and takes out papers. The Pastor comes in, he takes a chair and sits near Laura by the desk.]

PASTOR. Good evening, sister. I have been away all day, as you know, and only just got back. Terrible things have been happening here.

LAURA. Yes, brother, never have I gone through such a night and such a day.

PASTOR. I see that you are none the worse for it all.

LAURA. No, God be praised, but think what might have happened!

PASTOR. Tell me one thing, how did it begin? I have heard so many different versions.

LAURA. It began with his wild idea of not being Bertha's father, and ended with his throwing the lighted lamp in my face.

PASTOR. But this is dreadful! It is fully developed insanity. And what is to be done now?

LAURA. We must try to prevent further violence and the doctor has sent to the hospital for a straightjacket. In the meantime I have sent a message to the Colonel, and I am now trying to straighten out the affairs of the household, which he has carried on in a most reprehensible manner.

PASTOR. This is a deplorable story, but I have always expected something of the sort. Fire and powder must end in an explosion. What have you got in the drawer there?

LAURA [Has pulled out a drawer in the desk]. Look, he has hidden everything here.

PASTOR [Looking into drawer]. Good Heavens, here is your doll and here is your christening cap and Bertha's rattle; and your letters; and the locket. [Wipes his eyes.] After all he must have loved you very dearly, Laura. I never kept such things!

LAURA. I believe he used to love me, but time—time changes so many things.

PASTOR. What is that big paper? The receipt for a grave! Yes, better the grave than the lunatic asylum! Laura, tell me, are you blameless in all this?

LAURA. I? Why should I be to blame because a man goes out of his mind?

PASTOR. Well, well, I shan't say anything. After all, blood is thicker than water.

LAURA. What do you dare to intimate?

PASTOR [Looking at her penetratingly]. Now, listen!

LAURA. Yes?

PASTOR. You can hardly deny that it suits you pretty well to be able to educate your child as you wish?

LAURA. I don't understand.

PASTOR. How I admire you!

LAURA. Me? H'm!

PASTOR. And I am to become the guardian of that free-thinker! Do you know I have always looked on him as a weed in our garden.

[Laura gives a short laugh, and then becomes suddenly serious.]

LAURA. And you dare say that to me—his wife?

PASTOR. You are strong, Laura, incredibly strong. You are like a fox in a trap, you would rather gnaw off your own leg than let yourself be caught! Like a master thief—no accomplice, not even your own conscience. Look at yourself in the glass! You dare not!

LAURA. I never use a looking glass!

PASTOR. No, you dare not! Let me look at your hand. Not a tell-tale blood stain, not a trace of insidious poison! A little innocent murder that the law cannot reach, an unconscious crime—unconscious! What a splendid idea! Do you hear how he is working up there? Take care! If that man gets loose he will make short work of you.

LAURA. You talk so much, you must have a bad conscience. Accuse me if you can!

PASTOR. I cannot.

LAURA. You see! You cannot, and therefore I am innocent. You take care of your ward, and I will take care of mine! Here's the doctor.

[Doctor comes in.]

LAURA [Rising]. Good evening, Doctor. You at least will help me, won't you? But unfortunately there is not much that can be done. Do you hear how he is carrying on up there? Are you convinced now?

DOCTOR. I am convinced that an act of violence has been committed, but the question now is whether that act of violence can be considered an outbreak of passion or madness.

PASTOR. But apart from the actual outbreak, you must acknowledge that he has "fixed ideas."

DOCTOR. I think that your ideas, Pastor, are much more fixed.

PASTOR. My settled views about the highest things are—

DOCTOR. We'll leave settled views out of this. Madam, it rests with you to decide whether your husband is guilty to the extent of imprisonment and fine or should be put in an asylum! How do you class his behavior?

LAURA. I cannot answer that now.

DOCTOR. That is to say you have no decided opinion as to what will be most advantageous to the interests of the family? What do you say, Pastor?

PASTOR. Well, there will be a scandal in either case. It is not easy to say.

LAURA. But if he is only sentenced to a fine for violence, he will be able to repeat the violence.

DOCTOR. And if he is sent to prison he will soon be out again. Therefore we consider it most advantageous for all parties that he should be immediately treated as insane. Where is the nurse?

LAURA. Why?

DOCTOR. She must put the straightjacket on the patient when I have talked to him and given the order! But not before. I have—the—garment out here. [Goes out into the hall rind returns with a large bundle.] Please ask the nurse to come in here.

[Laura rings.]

PASTOR. Dreadful! Dreadful!

[Nurse comes in.]

DOCTOR [Takes out the straightjacket]. I want you to pay attention to this. We want you to slip this jacket on the Captain, from behind, you understand, when I find it necessary to prevent another outbreak of violence. You notice it has very long sleeves to prevent his moving and they are to be tied at the back. Here are two straps that go through buckles which are afterwards fastened to the arm of a chair or the sofa or whatever is convenient. Will you do it?

NURSE. No, Doctor, I can't do that; I can't.

LAURA. Why don't you do it yourself, Doctor?

DOCTOR. Because the patient distrusts me. You, Madam, would seem to be the one to do it, but I fear he distrusts even you.

[Laura's face changes for an instant.]

DOCTOR. Perhaps you, Pastor—

PASTOR. No, I must ask to be excused.

[Noejd comes in.]

LAURA. Have you delivered the message already?

NOEJD. Yes, Madam.

DOCTOR. Oh, is it you, Noejd? You know the circumstances here; you know that the Captain is out of his mind and you must help us to take care of him.

NOEJD. If there is anything I can do for the Captain, you may be sure I will do it.

DOCTOR. You must put this jacket on him—

NURSE. No, he shan't touch him. Noejd might hurt him. I would rather do it myself, very, very gently. But Noejd can wait outside and help me if necessary. He can do that.

[There is loud knocking on the private door.]

DOCTOR. There he is! Put the jacket under your shawl on the chair, and you must all go out for the time being and the Pastor and I will receive him, for that door will not hold out many minutes. Now go.

NURSE [Going out left.] The Lord help us!

[Laura locks desk, then goes out left. Noejd goes out back. After a moment the private door is forced open, with such violence that the lock is broken and the chair is thrown into the middle of the room. The Captain comes in with a pile of books under his arm, which he puts on the table.]

CAPTAIN. The whole thing is to be read here, in every book. So I wasn't out of my mind after all! Here it is in the Odyssey, book first, verse 215, page 6 of the Upsala translation. It is Telemachus speaking to Athene. "My mother indeed maintains that he, Odysseus, is my father, but I myself know it not, for no man yet hath known his own origin." And this suspicion is harbored by Telemachus about Penelope, the most virtuous of women! Beautiful, eh? And here we have the prophet Ezekiel: "The fool saith; behold here is my father, but who can tell whose loins engendered him." That's quite clear! And what have we here? The History of Russian Literature by Merslaekow. Alexander Puschkin, Russia's greatest poet, died of torture front the reports circulated about his wife's unfaithfulness rather than by the bullet in his breast, from a duel. On his deathbed he swore she was innocent. Ass, ass! How could he swear to it? You see, I read my books. Ah, Jonas, art you here? and the doctor, naturally. Have you heard what I answered when an English lady complained about Irishmen who used to throw lighted lamps in their wives' faces? "God, what women," I cried. "Women," she gasped. "Yes, of course," I answered. "When things go so far that a man, a man who loved and worshipped a woman, takes a lighted lamp and throws it in her face, then one may know."

PASTOR. Know what?

CAPTAIN. Nothing. One never knows anything. One only believes. Isn't that true, Jonas? One believes and then one is saved! Yes, to be sure. No, I know that one can be damned by his faith. I know that.

DOCTOR. Captain!

CAPTAIN. Silence! I don't want to talk to you; I won't listen to you repeating their chatter in there, like a telephone! In there! You know! Look here, Jonas; do you believe that you are the father of your children? I remember that you had a tutor in your house who had a handsome face, and the people gossiped about him.

PASTOR. Adolf, take care!

CAPTAIN. Grope under your toupee and feel if there are not two bumps there. By my soul, I believe he turns pale! Yes, yes, they will talk; but, good Lord, they talk so much. Still we are a lot of ridiculous dupes, we married men. Isn't that true, Doctor? How was it with your marriage bed? Didn't you have a lieutenant in the house, eh? Wait a moment and I will make a guess—his name was—[whispers in the Doctor's ear]. You see he turns pale, too! Don't be disturbed. She is dead and buried and what is done can't be undone. I knew him well, by the way, and he is now—look at me, Doctor—No, straight in my eyes—a major in the cavalry! By God, if I don't believe he has horns, too.

DOCTOR [Tortured]. Captain, won't you talk about something else?

CAPTAIN. Do you see? He immediately wants to talk of something else when I mention horns.

PASTOR. Do you know, Adolf, that you are insane?

CAPTAIN. Yes; I know that well enough. But if I only had the handling of your illustrious brains for awhile I'd soon have you shut up, too! I am mad, but how did I become so? That doesn't concern you, and it doesn't concern anyone. But you want to talk of something else now. [Takes the photograph album from the table.] Good Lord, that is my child! Mine? We can never know. Do you know what we would have to do to make sure? First, one should marry to get the respect of society, then be divorced soon after and become lovers, and finally adopt the children. Then one would at least be sure that they were one's adopted children. Isn't that right? But how can all that help us now? What can keep me now that you have taken my conception of immortality from me, what use is science and philosophy to me when I have nothing to live for, what can I do with life when I am dishonored? I grafted my right arm, half my brain, half my marrow on another trunk, for I believed they would knit themselves together and grow into a more perfect tree, and then someone came with a knife and cut below the graft, and now I am only half a tree. But the other half goes on growing with my arm and half my brain, while I wither and die, for they were the best parts I gave away. Now I want to die. Do with me as you will. I am no more.

[Buries his head on his arms on table. The Doctor whispers to the Pastor, and they go out through the door left. Soon after Bertha comes in.]

BERTRA [Goes up to Captain]. Are you ill, Father?

CAPTAIN [Looks up dazed]. I?

BERTHA. Do you know what you have done? Do you know that you threw the lamp at Mother?

CAPTAIN. Did I?

BERTHA. Yes, you did. Just think if she had been hurt.

CAPTAIN. What would that have mattered?

BERTHA. You are not my father when you talk like that.

CAPTAIN. What do you say? Am I not your father? How do you know that? Who told you that? And who is your father, then? Who?

BERTHA. Not you at any rate.

CAPTAIN. Still not I? Who, then? Who? You seem to be well informed. Who told you? That I should live to see my child come and tell me to my face that I am not her father! But don't you know that you disgrace your mother when you say that? Don't you know that it is to her shame if it is so?

BERTHA. Don't say anything bad about Mother; do you hear?

CAPTAIN. No; you hold together, every one of you, against me! and you have always done so.

BERTHA. Father!

CAPTAIN. Don't use that word again!

BERTHA. Father, father!

CAPTAIN [Draws her to him]. Bertha, dear, dear child, you are my child! Yes, Yes; it cannot be otherwise. It is so. The other was only sickly thoughts that come with the wind like pestilence and fever.

71

Look at me that I may see my soul in your eyes!—But I see her soul, too! You have two souls and you love me with one and hate me with the other. But you must only love me! You must have only one soul, or you will never have peace, nor I either. You must have only one mind, which is the child of my mind and one will, which is my will.

BERTHA. But I don't want to, I want to be myself.

CAPTAIN. You must not. You see, I am a cannibal, and I want to eat you. Your mother wanted to eat me, but she was not allowed to. I am Saturn who ate his children because it had been prophesied that they would eat him. To eat or be eaten! That is the question. If I do not eat you, you will eat me, and you have already shown your teeth! But don't be frightened my dear child; I won't harm you. [Goes and takes a revolver from the wall.]

BERTHA [Trying to escape]. Help, Mother, help, he wants to kill me.

NURSE [Comes in]. Mr. Adolf, what is it?

CAPTAIN [Examining revolver]. Have you taken out the cartridges?

NURSE. Yes, I put them away when I was tidying up, but sit down and be quiet and I'll get them out again!

[She takes the Captain by the arm and gets him into a chair, into which he sinks feebly. Then she takes out the straitjacket and goes behind the chair. Bertha slips out left.]

NURSE. Mr. Adolf, do you remember when you were my dear little boy and I tucked you in at night and used to repeat: "God who holds his children dear" to you, and do you remember how I used to get up in the night and give you a drink, how I would light the candle and tell you stories when you had bad dreams and couldn't sleep? Do you remember all that?

CAPTAIN. Go on talking, Margret, it soothes my head so. Tell me some more.

NURSE. O yes, but you must listen then! Do you remember when you took the big kitchen knife and wanted to cut out boats with it, and how I came in and had to get the knife away by fooling you? You were just a little child who didn't understand, so I had to fool you, for you didn't know that it was for your own good. "Give me that snake," I said, "or it will bite you!" and then you let go of the knife. [Takes the revolver out of the Captain's hand.] And then when you had to be dressed and didn't want to, I had to coax you and say that you should have a coat of gold and be dressed like a prince. And then I took your little blouse that was just made of green wool and held it in front of you and said: "In with both arms," and then I said, "Now sit nice and still while I button it down the back," [She puts the straightjacket on] and then I said, "Get up now, and walk across the floor like a good boy so I can see how it fits." [She leads him to the sofa.] And then I said, "Now you must go to bed."

CAPTAIN. What did you say? Was I to go to bed when I was dressed—damnation! what have you done to me? [Tries to get free.] Ah! you cunning devil of a woman! Who would have thought you had so much wit. [Lies down on sofa.] Trapped, shorn, outwitted, and not to be able to die!

NURSE. Forgive me, Mr. Adolf, forgive me, but I wanted to keep you from killing your child.

CAPTAIN. Why didn't you let me? You say life is hell and death the kingdom of heaven, and children belong to heaven.

NURSE. How do you know what comes after death?

CAPTAIN. That is the only thing we do know, but of life we know nothing! Oh, if one had only known from the beginning.

NURSE. Mr. Adolf, humble your hard heart and cry to God for mercy; it is not yet too late. It was not too late for the thief on the cross, when the Saviour said, "Today shalt thou be with me in Paradise."

CAPTAIN. Are you croaking for a corpse already, you old crow?

[Nurse takes a hymnbook out of her pocket.]

CAPTAIN [Calls]. Noejd, is Noejd out there?

[Noejd comes in.]

CAPTAIN. Throw this woman out! She wants to suffocate me with her hymn-book. Throw her out of the window, or up the chimney, or anywhere.

NOEJD. [Looks at Nurse]. Heaven help you, Captain, but I can't do that, I can't. If it were only six men, but a woman!

CAPTAIN. Can't you manage one woman, eh?

NOEJD. Of course I can,—but—well, you see, it's queer, but one never wants to lay hands on a woman.

CAPTAIN. Why not? Haven't they laid hands on me?

NOEJD. Yes, but I can't, Captain. It's just as if you asked me to strike the Pastor. It's second nature, like religion, I can't!

[Laura comes in, she motions Noejd to go.]

CAPTAIN. Omphale, Omphale! Now you play with the club while Hercules spins your wool.

LAURA [Goes to sofa]. Adolf, look at me. Do you believe that I am your enemy?

CAPTAIN. Yes, I do. I believe that you are all my enemies! My mother was my enemy when she did not want to bring me into the world because I was to be born with pain, and she robbed my embryonic life of its nourishment, and made a weakling of me. My sister was my enemy when she taught me that I must be submissive to her. The first woman I embraced was my enemy, for she gave me ten years of illness in return for the love I gave her. My daughter became my enemy when she had to choose between me and you. And you, my wife, you have been my arch enemy, because you never let up on me till I lay here lifeless.

LAURA. I don't know that. I ever thought or even intended what you think I did. It may be that a dim desire to get rid of you as an obstacle lay at the bottom of it, and if you see any design in my

74

behavior, it is possible that it existed, although I was unconscious of it. I have never thought how it all came about, but it is the result of the course you yourself laid out, and before God and my conscience I feel that I am innocent, even if I am not. Your existence has lain like a stone on my heart—lain so heavily that I tried to shake off the oppressive burden. This is the truth, and if I have unconsciously struck you down, I ask your forgiveness.

CAPTAIN. All that sounds plausible. But how does it help me? And whose fault is it? Perhaps spiritual marriages! Formerly one married a wife, now, one enters into partnership with a business woman, or goes to live with a friend—and then one ruins the partner, and dishonors the friend!—What has become of love, healthy sensuous love? It died in the transformation. And what is the result of this love in shares, payable to the bearer without joint liability? Who is the bearer when the crash comes? Who is the fleshly father of the spiritual child?

LAURA. And as for your suspicions about the child, they are absolutely groundless.

CAPTAIN. That's just what makes it so horrible. If at least there were any grounds for them, it would be something to get hold of, to cling to. Now there are only shadows that hide themselves in the bushes, and stick out their heads and grin; it is like fighting with the air, or firing blank cartridges in a sham fight. A fatal reality would have called forth resistance, stirred life and soul to action; but now my thoughts dissolve into air, and my brain grinds a void until it is on fire.—Put a pillow under my head, and throw something over me, I am cold. I am terribly cold!

[Laura takes her shawl and spreads it over him. Nurse goes to get a pillow.]

LAURA. Give me your hand, friend.

CAPTAIN. My band! The hand that you have bound! Omphale! Omphale!—But I feel your shawl against my mouth; it is as warm and soft as your arm, and it smells of vanilla, like your hair when you were young! Laura, when you were young, and we walked in the birch woods, with the primroses and the thrushes—glorious,

glorious! Think how beautiful life was, and what it is now. You didn't want to have it like this, nor did I, and yet it happened. Who then rules over life?

LAURA. God alone rules—

CAPTAIN. The God of strife then! Or the Goddess perhaps, nowadays.—Take away the cat that is lying on me! Take it away!

[Nurse brings in a pillow and takes the shawl away.]

CAPTAIN. Give me my army coat!—Throw it over me! [Nurse gets the coat and puts it over him.] Ah, my rough lion skin that, you wanted to take away from me! Omphale! Omphale! You cunning woman, champion of peace and contriver of man's disarmament. Wake, Hercules, before they take your club away from you! You would wile our armor from us too, and make believe that it is nothing but glittering finery. No, it was iron, let me tell you, before it ever glittered. In olden days the smith made the armor, now it is the needle woman. Omphale! Omphale! Rude strength has fallen before treacherous weakness. Out on you infernal woman, and damnation on your sex! [He raises himself to spit but falls back on the sofa.] What have you given me for a pillow, Margret? It is so hard, and so cold, so cold. Come and sit near me. There. May I put my head on your knee? So!—This is warm! Bend over me so that I can feel your breast! Oh, it is sweet to sleep against a woman's breast, a mother's, or a mistress's, but the mother's is sweetest.

LAURA. Would you like to see your child, Adolf?

CAPTAIN. My child? A man has no children, it is only woman who has children, and therefore the future is hers when we die childless. Oh, God, who holds his children dear!

NURSE. Listen, he is praying to God.

CAPTAIN. No, to you to put me to sleep, for I am tired, so tired. Good night, Margret, and blessed be you among women.

[He raises himself, but falls with a cry on the nurses's lap. Laura goes to left and calls the Doctor who comes in with the Pastor.]

LAURA. Help us, Doctor, if it isn't too late. Look, he has stopped breathing.

DOCTOR [Feels the Captain's pulse.] It is a stroke.

PASTOR. Is he dead?

DOCTOR. No, he may yet cone back to life, but to what an awakening we cannot tell.

PASTOR. "First death, and then the judgment."

DOCTOR. No judgment, and no accusations, you who believe that a God shapes man's destiny must go to him about this.

NURSE. Ah, Pastor, with his last breath he prayed to God.

PASTOR [To Laura]. Is that true?

LAURA. It is.

DOCTOR. In that case, which I can understand as little as the cause of his illness, my skill is at an end. You try yours now, Pastor.

LAURA. Is that all you have to say at this death-bed, Doctor?

DOCTOR. That is all! I know no more. Let him speak who knows more.

[Bertha comes in from left and runs to her mother.]

BERTHA. Mother, Mother!

LAURA. My child, my own child!

PASTOR. Amen.

CURTAIN.

COUNTESS JULIE

CHARACTERS
> COUNTESS JULIE, twenty-five years old
> JEAN, a valet, thirty
> KRISTIN, a cook, thirty-five
> FARM SERVANTS

The action takes place on Saint John's night, the mid-summer festival surviving from pagan times.

[SCENE.—A large kitchen. The ceiling and walls are partially covered by draperies and greens. The back wall slants upward from left side of scene. On back wall, left, are two shelves filled with copper kettles, iron casseroles and tin pans. The shelves are trimmed with fancy scalloped paper. To right of middle a large arched entrance with glass doors through which one sees a fountain with a statue of Cupid, syringa bushes in bloom and tall poplars. To left corner of scene a large stove with hood decorated with birch branches. To right, servants' dining table of white pine and a few chairs. On the cud of table stands a Japanese jar filled with syringa blossoms. The floor is strewn with juniper branches.]
[Near stove, an ice-box, sink and dish-table. A large old-fashioned bell, hangs over the door, to left of door a speaking tube.]
[Kristin stands at stork engaged in cooking something. She wears a light cotton dress and kitchen apron. Jean comes in wearing livery; he carries a large pair of riding-boots with spurs, which he puts on floor.]

JEAN. Tonight Miss Julie is crazy again, perfectly crazy.

KRISTIN. So—you're back at last.

JEAN. I went to the station with the Count and coming back I went in to the barn and danced and then I discovered Miss Julie there leading the dance with the gamekeeper. When she spied me, she rushed right toward me and asked me to waltz, and then she waltzed so—never in my life have I seen anything like it! Ah—she is crazy tonight.

KRISTIN. She has always been. But never so much as in the last fortnight, since her engagement was broken off.

JEAN. Yes, what about that gossip? He seemed like a fine fellow although he wasn't rich! Ach! they have so much nonsense about them. [Seats himself at table.] It's queer about Miss Julie though— to prefer staying here at home among these people, eh, to going away with her father to visit her relatives, eh?

KRISTIN. She's probably shamefaced about breaking off with her intended.

JEAN. No doubt! but he was a likely sort just the same. Do you know, Kristin, how it happened? I saw it, although I didn't let on.

KRISTIN. No—did you see it?

JEAN. Yes, indeed, I did. They were out in the stable yard one evening and she was "training" him as she called it. Do you know what happened? She made him leap over her riding whip, the way you teach a dog to jump. He jumped it twice and got a lash each time; but the third time he snatched the whip from her hand and broke it into pieces. And then he vanished!

KRISTIN. Was that the way it happened? No, you don't say so!

JEAN. Yes, that's the way the thing happened. But what have you got to give me that's good, Kristin?

KRISTIN. [She takes things from the pans on stove and serves them to him.] Oh, it's only a bit of kidney that I cut out of the veal steak for you.

JEAN [Smelling the food]. Splendid! My favorite delicacy. [Feeling of plate]. But you might have warmed the plate.

KRISTIN. You're fussier than the Count, when you get started. [Tweaks his hair.]

JEAN. Don't pull my hair! You know how sensitive I am.

KRISTIN. Oh—there, there! you know I was only loving you.

[Jean eats, and Kristin opens bottle of beer.]

JEAN. Beer on midsummer night—thank you, no! I have something better than that myself. [Takes bottle of wine from drawer of table.] Yellow seal, how's that? Now give me a glass—a wine glass you understand, of course, when one drinks the genuine.

KRISTIN. [Fetches a glass. Then goes to stove and puts on casserole.] Heaven help the woman who gets you for her husband. Such a fuss budget!

JEAN. Oh, talk! You ought to be glad to get such a fine fellow as I am. And I don't think it's done you any harm because I'm considered your intended. [Tastes wine.] Excellent, very excellent! Just a little too cold. [Warms glass with hands]. We bought this at Dijon. It stood at four francs a litre in the bulk; then of course there was the duty besides. What are you cooking now that smells so infernally?

KRISTIN. Oh, it's some devil's mess that Miss Julie must have for Diana.

JEAN. Take care of your words, Kristin. But why should you stand there cooking for that damned dog on a holiday evening? Is it sick, eh?

KRISTIN. Yes, it's sick. Diana sneaked out with the gatekeeper's mongrels and now something is wrong. Miss Julie can't stand that.

JEAN. Miss Julie has a great deal of pride about some things—but not enough about others! Just like her mother in her lifetime; she thrived best in the kitchen or the stable, but she must always drive tandem—never one horse! She would go about with soiled cuffs but she had to have the Count's crest on her cuff buttons. And as for Miss Julie, she doesn't take much care of her appearance either. I should say she isn't refined. Why just now out there she pulled the forester from Anna's side and asked him to dance with her. We wouldn't do things that way. But when the highborn wish to unbend they become vulgar. Splendid she is though! Magnificent! Ah, such shoulders and—

KRISTIN. Oh, don't exaggerate. I've heard what Clara says who dresses her sometimes, I have.

JEAN. Ha! Clara—you women are always jealous of each other. I who've been out riding with her—!!! And such a dancer!

KRISTIN. Come now, Jean, don't you want to dance with me when I'm through?

JEAN. Of course I want to.

KRISTIN. That is a promise?

JEAN. Promise! When I say I will do a thing I do it! Thanks for the supper—it was excellent.

[Pushes cork in the bottle with a bang. Miss Julie appears
in doorway, speaking to someone outside.]

JULIE. I'll be back soon, but don't let things wait for me.

[Jean quickly puts bottle in table drawer and rises
very respectfully.]

[Enter Miss Julie and goes to Kristin.]

JULIE. Is it done?

[Kristin indicating Jean's presence.]

JEAN [Gallantly]. Have you secrets between you?

JULIE. [Flipping handkerchief in his face]. Curious, are you?

JEAN. How sweet that violet perfume is!

81

JULIE [Coquettishly]. Impudence! Do you appreciate perfumes too? Dance—that you can do splendidly. [Jean looks towards the cooking store]. Don't look. Away with you.

JEAN [Inquisitive but polite]. Is it some troll's dish that you are both concocting for midsummer night? Something to pierce the future with and evoke the face of your intended?

JULIE [Sharply]. To see him one must have sharp eyes. [To Kristin]. Put it into a bottle and cork it tight. Come now, Jean and dance a schottische with me.

[Jean hesitates.]

JEAN. I don't wish to be impolite to anyone but—this dance I promised to Kristin.

JULIE. Oh, she can have another—isn't that so, Kristin? Won't you lend Jean to me.

KRISTIN. It's not for me to say, if Miss Julie is so gracious it's not for me to say no. [To Jean]. Go you and be grateful for the honor.

JEAN. Well said—but not wishing any offense I wonder if it is prudent for Miss Julie to dance twice in succession with her servant, especially as people are never slow to find meaning in—

JULIE [Breaking out]. In what? What sort of meaning? What were you going to say?

JEAN [Taken aback]. Since Miss Julie does not understand I must speak plainly. It may look strange to prefer one of your—underlings—to others who covet the same honor—

JULIE. To prefer—what a thought! I, the lady of the house! I honor the people with my presence and now that I feel like dancing I want to have a partner who knows how to lead to avoid being ridiculous.

JEAN. As Miss Julie commands. I'm here to serve.

JULIE [Mildly]. You mustn't look upon that as a command. Tonight we are all in holiday spirits—full of gladness and rank is flung aside.

So, give me your arm! Don't be alarmed, Kristin, I shall not take your sweetheart away from you.

[Jean offers arm. They exit.]

[PANTOMIME.—Played as though the actress were really alone. Turns her back to the audience when necessary. Does not look out into the auditorium. Does not hurry as though fearing the audience might grow restless. Soft violin music from the distance, schottische time. Kristin hums with the music. She cleans the table; washes plate, wipes it and puts it in the china closet. Takes off her apron and then opens drawer of table and takes a small hand glass and strands it against a flower pot on table. Lights a candle and heats a hair pin with which she crimps her hair around her forehead. After that she goes to door at back and listens. Then she returns to table and sees the Countess' handkerchief, picks it up, smells of it, then smooths it out and folds it. Enter Jean.]

JEAN. She is crazy I tell you! To dance like that! And the people stand grinning at her behind the doors. What do you say to that, Kristin?

KRISTIN. Oh, didn't I say she's been acting queer lately? But isn't it my turn to dance now?

JEAN. You are not angry because I let myself be led by the forelock?

KRISTIN. No, not for such a little thing. That you know well enough. And I know my place too—

JEAN [Puts arm around her waist]. You're a pretty smart girl, Kristin, and you ought to make a good wife.

[Enter Miss Julie.]

JULIE [Disagreeably surprised, but with forced gaiety]. You're a charming cavalier to run away from your partner.

JEAN. On the contrary, Miss Julie, I have hastened to my neglected one as you see.

JULIE [Changing subject]. Do you know, you dance wonderfully well! But why are you in livery on a holiday night? Take it off immediately.

JEAN. Will you excuse me—my coat hangs there. [Goes R. and takes coat.]

JULIE. Does it embarrass you to change your coat in my presence? Go to your room then—or else stay and I'll turn my back.

JEAN. With your permission, Miss Julie.

[Exit Jean R. One sees his arm as he changes coat.]

JULIE [To Kristin]. Is Jean your sweetheart, that he is so devoted?

KRISTIN. Sweetheart? Yes, may it please you. Sweetheart—that's what they call it.

JULIE. Call it?

KRISTIN. Oh Miss Julie has herself had a sweetheart and—

JULIE. Yes, we were engaged—

KRISTIN. But it came to nothing.

[Enter Jean in black frock coat.]

JULIE. Tres gentil, Monsieur Jean, tres gentil.

JEAN. Vous voulez plaisanter, Mademoiselle.

JULIE. Et vous voulez parler francais? Where did you learn that?

JEAN. In Switzerland where I was butler in the largest hotel at Lucerne.

JULIE. Why, you look like a gentleman in your frock coat. Charmant! [Seats herself by table.]

JEAN. You flatter me!

JULIE. Flatter! [Picking him up on the word.]

JEAN. My natural modesty forbids me to believe that you could mean these pleasant things that you say to a—such its I am—and therefore I allowed myself to fancy that you overrate or, as it is called, flatter.

JULIE. Where did you learn to use words like that? Have you frequented the theatres much?

JEAN. I have frequented many places, I have!

JULIE. But you were born here in this neighborhood?

JEAN. My father was a deputy under the public prosecutor, and I saw Miss Julie as a child—although she didn't see me!

JULIE. No, really?

JEAN. Yes, I remember one time in particular. But I mustn't talk about that.

JULIE. Oh yes, do, when was it?

JEAN. No really—not now, another time perhaps.

JULIE. "Another time" is a good for nothing. Is it so dreadful then?

JEAN. Not dreadful—but it goes against the grain. [Turns and points to Kristin, who has fallen asleep in a chair near stove]. Look at her.

JULIE. She'll make a charming wife! Does she snore too?

JEAN. No, but she talks in her sleep.

JULIE [Cynically]. How do you know that she talks in her sleep?

JEAN [Boldly]. I have heard her.[Pause and they look at each other.]

JULIE. Why don't you sit down?

JEAN. I can't allow myself to do so in your presence.

JULIE. But if I command you?

JEAN. Then I obey.

JULIE. Sit down then. But wait—can't you get me something to drink first?

JEAN. I don't know what there is in the icebox. Nothing but beer, probably.

JULIE. Is beer nothing? My taste is so simple that I prefer it to wine.

[Jean takes out beer and serves it on plate.]

JEAN. Allow me.

JULIE. Won't you drink too?

JEAN. I am no friend to beer—but if Miss Julie commands.

JULIE [Gaily]. Commands! I should think as a polite cavalier you might join your lady.

JEAN. Looking at it in that way you are quite right. [Opens another bottle of beer and fills glass.]

JULIE. Give me a toast!

[Jean hesitates.]

JULIE [Mockingly]. Old as he is, I believe the man is bashful!

JEAN [On his knee with mock gallantry, raises glass]. A health to my lady of the house!

JULIE. Bravo! Now you must kiss my slipper. Then the thing is perfect.

[Jean hesitates and then seizes her foot and kisses it lightly.]

JULIE. Splendid! You should have been an actor.

JEAN [Rising]. But this mustn't go any further, Miss Julie. What if someone should come in and see us?

JULIE. What harm would that do?

JEAN. Simply that it would give them a chance to gossip. And if Miss Julie only knew how their tongues wagged just now—then—

JULIE. What did they say? Tell me. And sit down now.

JEAN [Sitting]. I don't wish to hurt you, but they used an expression—threw hints of a certain kind—but you are not a child, you can understand. When one sees a lady drinking alone with a man—let alone a servant—at night—then—

JULIE. Then what? And for that matter, we are not alone. Kristin is here.

JEAN. Sleeping! Yes.

JULIE. Then I shall wake her. [Rises]. Kristin, are you asleep?

KRISTIN. [In her sleep]. Bla—bla—bla—bla.

JULIE. Kristin! She certainly can sleep. [Goes to Kristin.]

KRISTIN. [In her sleep]. The Count's boots are polished—put on the coffee—soon—soon—soon. Oh—h-h-h—puh! [Breathes heavily. Julie takes her by the nose.]

JULIE. Won't you wake up?

JEAN [Sternly]. Don't disturb the sleeping.

JULIE [Sharply]. What?

JEAN. Anyone who has stood over the hot stove all day long is tired when night comes. One should respect the weary.

JULIE. That's a kind thought—and I honor it. [Offers her hand.] Thanks for the suggestion. Come out with me now and pick some syringas.

[Kristin has awakened and goes to her room, right, in a sort of sleep stupified way.]

JEAN. With Miss Julie?

JULIE. With me.

JEAN. But that wouldn't do—decidedly not.

JULIE. I don't understand you. Is it possible that you fancy that I—

JEAN. No—not I, but people.

JULIE. What? That I'm in love with my coachman?

JEAN. I am not presumptuous, but we have seen instances—and with the people nothing is sacred.

JULIE. I believe he is an aristocrat!

JEAN. Yes, I am.

JULIE. But I step down—

JEAN. Don't step down, Miss Julie. Listen to me—no one would believe that you stepped down of your own accord; people always say that one falls down.

JULIE. I think better of the people than you do. Come—and try them—come!

[Dares him with a look.]

JEAN. Do you know that you are wonderful?

JULIE. Perhaps. But you are too. Everything is wonderful for that matter. Life, people—everything. Everything is wreckage, that drifts over the water until it sinks, sinks. I have the same dream every now and then and at this moment I am reminded of it. I find myself seated at the top of a high pillar and I see no possible way to get down. I grow dizzy when I look down, but down I must. But I'm not brave enough to throw myself; I cannot hold fast and I long to fall—but I don't fall. And yet I can find no rest or peace until I shall come down to earth; and if I came down to earth I would wish myself down in the ground. Have you ever felt like that?

JEAN. No, I dream that I'm lying in a dark wood under a tall tree and I would up—up to the top, where I can look far over the fair landscape, where the sun is shining. I climb—climb, to plunder the birds' nests up there where the golden eggs lie, but the tree trunk is so thick, so smooth, and the first limb is so high! But I know if I reached the first limb I should climb as though on a ladder, to the top. I haven't reached it yet, but I shall reach it, if only in the dream.

JULIE. Here I stand talking about dreams with you. Come now, just out in the park.

[She offers her arm and they start.]

JEAN. We should sleep on nine midsummer flowers tonight and then our dreams would come true.

[She turns, Jean quickly holds a hand over his eye.]

JULIE. What is it, something in your eye?

JEAN. Oh, it is nothing—just a speck. It will be all right in a moment.

JULIE. It was some dust from my sleeve that brushed against you. Now sit down and let me look for it. [Pulls him into a chair, looks into his eye.] Now sit still, perfectly still. [Uses corner of her handkerchief in his eye. Strikes his hand.] So—will you mind? I believe you are trembling, strong man that you are. [Touching his arm.] And such arms!

JEAN [Warningly.] Miss Julie!

JULIE. Yes, Monsieur Jean!

JEAN. Attention. Je ne suis qu'un homme! I am a man

JULIE. Will you sit Still! So, now it is gone! Kiss my hand and thank me!

[Jean rises.]

JEAN. Miss Julie, listen to me. Kristin has gone to bed now—will you listen to me—

JULIE. Kiss my hand first.

JEAN. Listen to me—

JULIE. Kiss my hand first.

JEAN. Yes, but blame yourself.

JULIE. For what?

JEAN. For what? Are you a child at twenty-five? Don't you know that it is dangerous to play with fire?

JULIE. Not for me. I am insured!

JEAN. No, you are not. But even if you are, there is inflammable material in the neighborhood.

JULIE. Might that be you?

JEAN. Yes, not because it is I, but because I'm a young man—

JULIE [Scornfully]. With a grand opportunity—what inconceivable presumption! A Don Juan perhaps! Or a Joseph! On my soul, I believe he is a Joseph!

JEAN. You do?

JULIE. Almost.

> [Jean rushes towards her and tries to take her in
> his arms to kiss her.]

JULIE [Gives him a box on the ear]. Shame on you.

JEAN. Are you in earnest, or fooling?

JULIE. In earnest.

JEAN. Then you were in earnest a moment ago, too. You play too seriously with what is dangerous. Now I'm tired of playing and beg to be excused that I may go on with my work. The Count must have his boots in time, and it is long past midnight. [Jean picks up boots.]

JULIE. Put those boots away.

JEAN. No, that is my work which it is my duty to do, but I was not hired to be your play thing and that I shall never be. I think too well of myself for that.

JULIE. You are proud.

JEAN. In some things—not in others.

JULIE. Were you ever in love?

JEAN. We do not use that word, but I have liked many girls. One time I was sick because I couldn't have the one I wanted—sick, you understand, like the princesses in the Arabian Nights who could not eat nor drink for love sickness.

JULIE. Who was she? [Jean is silent.] Who was she?

JEAN. That you could not make me tell.

JULIE. Not if I ask you as an equal, as a—friend? Who was she?

JEAN. It was you!

[Julie seats herself.]

JULIE. How extravagant!

JEAN. Yes, if you will, it was ridiculous. That was the story I hesitated to tell, but now I'm going to tell it. Do you know how people in high life look from the under world? No, of course you don't. They look like hawks and eagles whose backs one seldom sees, for they soar up above. I lived in a hovel provided by the state, with seven brothers and sisters and a pig; out on a barren stretch where nothing grew, not even a tree, but from the window I could see the Count's park walls with apple trees rising above them. That was the garden of paradise; and there stood many angry angels with flaming swords protecting it; but for all that I and other boys found the way to the tree of life—now you despise me.

JULIE. Oh, all boys steal apples.

JEAN. You say that, but you despise me all the same. No matter! One time I entered the garden of paradise—it was to weed the onion beds with my mother! Near the orchard stood a Turkish

91

pavilion, shaded and overgrown with jessamine and honeysuckle. I didn't know what it was used for and I had never seen anything so beautiful. People passed in and out and one day—the door was left open. I sneaked in and beheld walls covered with pictures of kings and emperors and there were red-fringed curtains at the windows—now you understand what I mean—I—[Breaks off a spray of syringes and puts it to her nostrils.] I had never been in the castle and how my thoughts leaped—and there they returned ever after. Little by little the longing came over me to experience for once the pleasure of—enfin, I sneaked in and was bewildered. But then I heard someone coming—there was only one exit for the great folk, but for me there was another, and I had to choose that. [Julie who has taken the syringa lets it fall on table.] Once out I started to run, scrambled through a raspberry hedge, rushed over a strawberry bed and came to a stop on the rose terrace. For there I saw a figure in a white dress and white slippers and stockings—it was you! I hid under a heap of weeds, under, you understand, where the thistles pricked me, and lay on the damp, rank earth. I gazed at you walking among the roses. And I thought if it is true that the thief on the cross could enter heaven and dwell among the angels it was strange that a pauper child on God's earth could not go into the castle park and play with the Countess' daughter.

JULIE [Pensively]. Do you believe that all poor children would have such thoughts under those conditions?

JEAN [Hesitates, then in a positive voice]. That all poor children—yes, of course, of course!

JULIE. It must be a terrible misfortune to be poor.

JEAN [With deep pain and great chagrin]. Oh, Miss Julie, a dog may lie on the couch of a Countess, a horse may be caressed by a lady's hand, but a servant—yes, yes, sometimes there is stuff enough in a man, whatever he be, to swing himself up in the world, but how often does that happen! But to return to the story, do you know what I did? I ran down to the mill dam and threw myself in with my clothes on—and was pulled out and got a thrashing. But the following Sunday when all the family went to visit my grandmother I contrived to stay at home; I scrubbed myself well, put on my best dollies, such its they were, and went to church so that I might see you. I saw you. Then I went home with my mind made up to put, an cud to myself. But I wanted to do it beautifully and without pain. Then I happened to remember that elderberry blossoms are poisonous. I knew where there was a big elderberry bush in full bloom and I stripped it of its riches and made a bed of it in the oat-bin. Have you ever noticed how smooth and glossy oats are? As soft as a woman's arm.—Well, I got in and let down the cover, fell asleep, and when I awoke I was very ill, but didn't die—as you see. What I wanted—I don't know. You were unattainable, but through the vision of you I was made to realize how hopeless it was to rise above the conditions of my birth.

JULIE. You tell it well! Were you ever at school?

JEAN. A little, but I have read a good deal and gone to the theatres. And besides, I have always heard the talk of fine folks and from them I have learned most.

JULIE. Do you listen then to what we are saying?

JEAN. Yes, indeed, I do. And I have heard much when I've been on the coachbox. One time I heard Miss Julie and a lady—

JULIE. Oh, what was it you heard?

JEAN. Hm! that's not so easy to tell. But I was astonished and could not understand where you had heard such things. Well, perhaps at bottom there's not so much difference between people and—people.

JULIE. Oh, shame! We don't behave as you do when we are engaged.

JEAN. [Eyeing her]. Are you sure of that? It isn't worthwhile to play the innocent with me.

JULIE. I gave my love to a rascal.

JEAN. That's what they always say afterward.

JULIE. Always?

JEAN. Always, I believe, as I have heard the expression many times before under the same circumstances.

JULIE. What circumstances?

JEAN. Those we've been talking about. The last time I—

JULIE. Silence. I don't wish to hear any more.

JEAN. Well, then I beg to be excused so I may go to bed.

JULIE. Go to bed! On midsummer night?

JEAN. Yes, for dancing out there with that pack has not amused me.

JULIE. Then get the key for the boat and row me out over the lake. I want to see the sun rise.

JEAN. Is that prudent?

JULIE. One would think that, you were afraid of your reputation.

JEAN. Why not? I don't want to be made ridiculous. I am not willing to be driven out without references, now that I am going to settle down. And I feel I owe something to Kristin.

JULIE. Oh, so it's Kristin now—

JEAN. Yes, but you too. Take my advice, go up and go to bed.

JULIE. Shall I obey you?

JEAN. For once—for your own sake. I beg of you. Night is crawling along, sleepiness makes one irresponsible and the brain grows hot. Go to your room. In fact—if I hear rightly some of the people are coming for me. If they find us here—then you are lost.

[Chorus is heard approaching, singing.]

"There came two ladies out of the woods
Tridiridi-ralla tridiridi-ra.
One of them had wet her foot,
Tridiridi-ralla-la.

"They talked of a hundred dollars,
Tridiridi-ralla tridiridi-ra.
But neither had hardly a dollar,
Tridiridi-ralla-la.

"The mitten I'm going to send you,
Tridirichi-ralla tridiridi-ra.
For another I'm going to jilt you,
Tridiridi-ralla tridiridi-ra."

JULIE. I know the people and I love them and they respect me. Let them come, you shall see.

JEAN. No, Miss Julie, they don't love you. They take your food and spit upon your kindness, believe me. Listen to them, listen to what they're singing! No! Don't listen!

JULIE [Listening]. What are they singing?

JEAN. It's something suggestive, about you and me.

JULIE. Infamous! Oh horrible! And how cowardly!

JEAN. The pack is always cowardly. And in such a battle one can only run away.

JULIE. Run away? Where? We can't get out and we can't go to Kristin.

JEAN. Into my room then. Necessity knows no law. You can depend on me for I am your real, genuine, respectful friend.

JULIE. But think if they found you there.

JEAN. I will turn the key and if they try to break in I'll shoot. Come—come!

JULIE. [Meaningly]. You promise me—?

JEAN. I swear . . .

[She exits R. Jean follows her.]

[BALLET.—The farm folk enter in holiday dress with flowers in their hats, a fiddler in the lead. They carry a keg of home-brewed beer and a smaller keg of gin, both decorated with greens which are placed on the table. They help themselves to glasses and drink. Then they sing and dance a country dance to the melody of "There came two ladies out of the woods." When that is over they go out, singing.]

[Enter Julie alone, sees the havoc the visitors have made, clasps her hands, takes out powder box and powders her face. Enter Jean exuberant.]

JEAN. There, you see, and you heard them. Do you think it's possible for us to remain here any longer?

JULIE. No, I don't. But what's to be done?

JEAN. Fly! Travel—far from here!

JULIE. Travel—yes—but where?

JEAN. To Switzerland—to the Italian lakes. You have never been there?

JULIE. No—is it beautiful there?

JEAN. Oh, an eternal summer! Oranges, trees, laurels—oh!

JULIE. But what shall we do there?

JEAN. I'll open a first-class hotel for first-class patrons.

JULIE. Hotel?

JEAN. That is life—you shall see! New faces constantly, different languages. Not a moment for boredom. Always something to do night and day—the bell ringing, the trains whistling, the omnibus coming and going and all the time the gold pieces rolling into the till—that is life!

JULIE. Yes, that is life. And I—?

JEAN. The mistress of the establishment—the ornament of the house. With your looks—and your manners—oh, it's a sure success! Colossal! You could sit like a queen in the office and set the slaves in action by touching an electric button. The guests line up before your throne and shyly lay their riches on your desk. You can't believe how people tremble when they get their bills—I can salt the bills and you can sweeten them with your most bewitching smile—ha, let us get away from here—[Takes a time table from his pocket] immediately—by the next train. We can be at Malmoe at 6.30, Hamburg at 8.40 tomorrow morning, Frankfort the day after and at Como by the St. Gothard route in about—let me see, three days. Three days!

JULIE. All that is well enough, but Jean—you must give me courage. Take me in your arms and tell me that you love me.

JEAN [Hesitatingly]. I will—but I daren't—not again in this house. I love you of course—do you doubt that?

JULIE [Shyly and with womanliness]. You! Say thou to me! Between us there can be no more formality. Say thou.

JEAN. I can't—There must be formality between us—as long as we are in this house. There is the memory of the past—and there is the Count, your father. I have never known anyone else for whom I have such respect. I need only to see his gloves lying in a chair to feel my own insignificance. I have only to hear his bell to start like a nervous horse—and now as I see his boots standing there so stiff and proper I feel like bowing and scraping. [Gives boots a kick]. Superstitions and prejudices taught in childhood can't be uprooted in a moment. Let us go to a country that is it republic where they'll stand on their heads for my coachman's livery—on their heads shall they stand—but I shall not. I am not, born to bow and scrape, for there's stuff in me—character. If I only get hold of the first limb, you shall see me climb. I'm a coachman today, but next year I shall be a proprietor, in two years a gentleman of income; then for Roumania where I'll let them decorate me and can, mark you, *can* end a count!

JULIE. Beautiful, beautiful!

JEAN. Oh, in Roumania, one can buy a title cheap—and so you can be a countess just the same—my countess!

JULIE. What do I care for all that—which I now cast behind me. Say that you love me—else, what am I, without it?

JEAN. I'll say it a thousand times afterwards, but not here. Above all, let us have no sentimentality now or everything will fall through. We must look at this matter coldly like sensible people. [Takes out a cigar and lights it.] Now sit down there and I'll sit here and we'll take it over as if nothing had happened.

JULIE [Staggered]. Oh, my God, have you no feeling?

JEAN. I? No one living has more feeling than I but I can restrain myself.

JULIE. A moment ago you could kiss my slipper and now—

JEAN [Harshly]. That was—then. Now we have other things to think about.

JULIE. Don't speak harshly to me.

JEAN. Not harshly, but wisely. One folly has been committed— commit no more. The Count may be here at any moment, and before he comes, our fate must be settled. How do my plans for the future strike you? Do you approve of them?

JULIE. They seem acceptable enough. But one question. For such a great undertaking a large capital is necessary, have you that?

JEAN [Chewing his cigar]. I? To be sure. I have my regular occupation, my unusual experience, my knowledge of different languages—that is capital that counts, I should say.

JULIE. But with all that you could not buy a railway ticket.

JEAN. That's true, and for that reason I'm looking for a backer who can furnish the funds.

JULIE. How can that be done at a moment's notice?

JEAN. That is for you to say, if you wish to be my companion.

JULIE. I can't—as I have nothing myself.

[A pause.]

JEAN. Then the whole matter drops—

JULIE. And—

JEAN. Things remain as they are.

JULIE. Do you think I could remain under this roof after—Do you think I will allow the people to point at me in scorn, or that I can ever look my father in the face again? Never! Take me away from this humiliation and dishonor. Oh, what have I done! Oh, my God, what have I done! [Weeping.]

JEAN. So, you are beginning in that tune now. What have you done? The same as many before you.

JULIE. And now you despise me. I am falling! I am falling!

JEAN. Fall down to my level, I'll lift you up afterwards.

JULIE. What strange power drew me to you—the weak to the strong—the falling to the rising, or is this love! This—love! Do you know what love is?

JEAN. I? Yes! Do you think it's the first time?

JULIE. What language, what thoughts.

JEAN. I am what life has made me. Don't be nervous and play the high and mighty, for now we are on the same level. Look here, my little girl, let me offer you a glass of something extra fine. [Opens drawer of table and takes out wine bottle, then fills two glasses that have been already used.]

JULIE. Where did you get that wine?

JEAN. From the cellar.

JULIE. My father's Burgundy.

JEAN. What's the matter, isn't that good enough for the son-in-law?

JULIE. And I drink beer—I!

JEAN. That only goes to prove that your taste is poorer than mine.

JULIE. Thief!

JEAN. Do you intend to tattle?

JULIE. Oh ho! Accomplice to a house thief. Was I intoxicated—have I been walking in my sleep this night—midsummer night, the night for innocent play—

JEAN. Innocent, eh!

JULIE [Pacing back and forth]. Is there a being on earth so miserable as I.

JEAN. Why are you, after such a conquest. Think of Kristin in there, don't you think she has feelings too?

JULIE. I thought so a little while ago, but I don't any more. A servant is a servant.

JEAN. And a whore is a whore.

JULIE [Falls on her knees with clasped hands]. Oh, God in heaven, end my wretched life, save me from this mire into which I'm sinking—Oh save me, save me.

JEAN. I can't deny that it hurts me to see you like this.

JULIE. And you who wanted to die for me.

JEAN. In the oat-bin? Oh, that was only talk.

JULIE. That is to say—a lie!

JEAN [Beginning to show sleepiness]. Er—er almost. I believe I read something of the sort in a newspaper about a chimney-sweep who made a death bed for himself of syringa blossoms in a wood-bin—[laughs] because they were going to arrest him for non-support of his children.

JULIE. So you are such a—

JEAN. What better could I have hit on! One must always be romantic to capture a woman.

JULIE. Wretch! Now you have seen the eagle's back, and I suppose I am to be the first limb—

JEAN. And the limb is rotten—

JULIE [Without seeming to hear]. And I am to be the hotel's signboard—

JEAN. And I the hotel—

JULIE. And sit behind the desk and allure guests and overcharge them—

JEAN. Oh, that'll be my business.

JULIE. That a soul can be so degraded!

JEAN. Look to your own soul.

JULIE. Lackey! Servant! Stand up when I speak.

JEAN. Don't you dare to moralize to me. Lackey, eh! Do you think you have shown yourself finer than any maid-servant tonight?

JULIE [Crushed]. That is right, strike me, trample on me, I deserve nothing better. I have done wrong, but help me now. Help me out of this if there is any possible way.

JEAN [Softens somewhat]. I don't care to shirk my share of the blame, but do you think any one of my position would ever have dared to raise his eyes to you if you yourself had not invited it? Even now I am astonished—

JULIE. And proud.

JEAN. Why not? Although I must confess that the conquest was too easy to be exciting.

JULIE. Go on, strike me again—

JEAN [Rising]. No, forgive me, rather, for what I said. I do not strike the unarmed, least of all, a woman. But I can't deny that from a certain point of view it gives me satisfaction to know that it is the glitter of brass, not gold, that dazzles us from below, and that the eagle's back is grey like the rest of him. On the other hand, I'm sorry to have to realize that all that I have looked up to is not worth while, and it pains me to see you fallen lower than your cook as it pains me to see autumn blossoms whipped to pieces by the cold rain and transformed into—dirt!

JULIE. You speak as though you were already my superior.

JEAN. And so I am! For I can make you a countess and you could never make me a count.

JULIE. But I am born of a count, that you can never be.

JEAN. That is true, but I can be the father of counts—if—

JULIE. But you are a thief—that I am not.

JEAN. There are worse things than that, and for that matter when I serve in a house I regard myself as a member of the family, a child of the house as it were. And one doesn't consider it theft if children snoop a berry from full bushes. [With renewed passion]. Miss Julie, you are a glorious woman—too good for such as I. You have been the victim of an infatuation and you want to disguise this fault by fancying that you love me. But you do not—unless perhaps my outer self attracts you. And then your love is no better than mine. But I cannot be satisfied with that, and your real love I can never awaken.

JULIE. Are you sure of that?

JEAN. You mean that we could get along with such an arrangement? There's no doubt about my loving you—you are beautiful, you are elegant—[Goes to her and takes her hand] accomplished, lovable when you wish to be, and the flame that you awaken in man does not die easily. [Puts arm around her.] You are like hot wine with strong spices, and your lips—

[Tries to kiss her. Julie pulls herself away slowly.]

JULIE. Leave me—I'm not to be won this way.

JEAN. How then? Not with caresses and beautiful words? Not by thoughts for the future, to save humiliation? How then?

JULIE. How? I don't know. I don't know! I shrink from you as I would from a rat. But I cannot escape from you.

JEAN. Escape with me.

JULIE. Escape? Yes, we must escape.—But I'm so tired. Give me a glass of wine. [Jean fills a glass with wine, Julie looks at her watch.] We must talk it over first for we have still a little time left.

[She empties the glass and puts it out for more.]

JEAN. Don't drink too much. It will go to your head.

JULIE. What harm will that do?

JEAN. What harm? It's foolish to get intoxicated. But what did you want to say?

JULIE. We must go away, but we must talk first. That is, I must speak, for until now you have done all the talking. You have told me about your life—now I will tell you about mine, then we will know each other through and through before we start on our wandering together.

JEAN. One moment, pardon. Think well whether you won't regret having told your life's secrets.

JULIE. Aren't you my friend?

JEAN. Yes. Sometimes. But don't depend on me.

JULIE. You only say that. And for that matter I have no secrets. You see, my mother was not of noble birth. She was brought up with ideas of equality, woman's freedom and all that. She had very decided opinions against matrimony, and when my father courted her she declared that she would never be his wife—but she did so for all that. I came into the world against my mother's wishes, I discovered, and was brought up like a child of nature by my mother, and taught everything that a boy must know as well; I was to be an example of a woman being as good as a man—I was made to go about in boy's clothes and take care of the horses and harness and saddle and hunt, and all such things; in fact, all over the estate women servants were taught to do men's work, with the result that the property came near being ruined—and so we became the laughing stock of the countryside. At last my father must have awakened from his bewitched condition, for he revolted, and ran things according to his ideas. My mother became ill—what it was I don't know, but she often had cramps and acted queerly—sometimes hiding in the attic or the orchard, and would even be gone all night at times. Then came the big fire which of course you have heard about. The house, the stables—everything was burned, under circumstances that pointed strongly to an incendiary, for the misfortune happened the day after the quarterly insurance was due and the premiums sent in by father were strangely delayed by his messenger so that they arrived too late. [She fills a wine glass and drinks.]

JEAN. Don't drink any more.

JULIE. Oh, what does it matter? My father was utterly at a loss to know where to get money to rebuild with. Then my mother suggested that he try to borrow from a man who had been her friend in her youth—a brick manufacturer here in the neighborhood. My father made the loan, but wasn't allowed to pay any interest, which suprised him. Then the house was rebuilt. [Julie drinks again.] Do you know who burned the house?

JEAN. Her ladyship, your mother?

JULIE. Do you know who the brick manufacturer was?

JEAN. Your mother's lover?

JULIE. Do you know whose money it was?

JEAN. Just a moment, that I don't know.

JULIE. It was my mother's.

JEAN. The Count's—that is to say, unless there was a contract.

JULIE. There was no contract. My mother had some money which she had not wished to have in my father's keeping and therefore, she had entrusted it to her friend's care.

JEAN. Who kept it.

JULIE. Quite right—he held on to it. All this came to my father's knowledge. He couldn't proceed against him, wasn't allowed to pay his wife's friend, and couldn't prove that it was his wife's money. That was my mother's revenge for his taking the reins of the establishment into his own hands. At that time he was ready to shoot himself. Gossip had it that he had tried and failed. Well, he lived it down—and my mother paid full penalty for her misdeed. Those were five terrible years for me, as you can fancy. I sympathized with my father, but I took my mother's part, for I didn't know the true circumstances. Through her I learned to distrust and hate men, and I swore to her never to be a man's slave.

JEAN. But you became engaged to the Lieutenant Governor.

JULIE. Just to make him my slave.

JEAN. But that he didn't care to be.

JULIE. He wanted to be, fast enough, but I grew tired of him.

JEAN. Yes—I noticed that—in the stable-yard!

JULIE. What do you mean?

JEAN. I saw how he broke the engagement.

JULIE. That's a lie. It was I who broke it. Did he say he broke it—the wretch!

JEAN. I don't believe that he was a wretch. You hate men, Miss Julie.

JULIE. Most of them. Sometimes one is weak—

JEAN. You hate me?

JULIE. Excessively. I could see you shot—

JEAN. Like a mad dog?

JULIE. Exactly!

JEAN. But there is nothing here to shoot with. What shall we do then?

JULIE [Rousing herself].We must get away from here—travel.

JEAN. And torture each other to death?

JULIE. No—to enjoy, a few days, a week—as long as we can. And then to die.

JEAN. Die! How silly. I think it's better to start the hotel.

JULIE [Not heeding him]. By the Lake of Como where the sun is always shining, where the laurel is green at Christmas and the oranges glow.

JEAN. The Lake of Como is it rain hole, I never saw any oranges there except on fruit stands. But it's a good resort, and there are many villas to rent to loving couples. That's a very paying industry. You know why? They take leases for half a year at least, but they usually leave in three weeks.

JULIE [Naively]. Why after three weeks?

JEAN. Why? They quarrel of course, but the rent must be paid all the same. Then you re-let, and so one after another they come and go, for there is plenty of love, although it doesn't last long.

JULIE. Then you don't want to die with me?

JEAN. I don't want to die at all, both because I enjoy living and because I regard suicide as a crime to Him who has given us life.

JULIE. Then you believe in God?

JEAN. Yes. Of course I do, and I go to church every other Sunday—But I'm tired of all this and I'm going to bed.

JULIE. Do you think I would allow myself to be satisfied with such an ending? Do you know what a man owes to a woman he hits—

JEAN [Takes out a silver coin and throws it on the table]. Allow me, I don't want to owe anything to anyone.

JULIE [Pretending not to notice the insult]. Do you know what the law demands?

JEAN. I know that the law demands nothing of a woman who seduces a man.

JULIE [Again not heeding him]. Do you see any way out of it but to travel?—wed—and separate?

JEAN. And if I protest against this misalliance?

JULIE. Misalliance!

JEAN. Yes, for me. For you see I have a finer ancestry than you, for I have no fire-bug in my family.

JULIE. How do you know?

JEAN. You can't prove the contrary. We have no family record except that which the police keep. But your pedigree I have read in a book on the drawing room table. Do you know who the founder of your family was? It was a miller whose wife found favor with the king during the Danish War. Such ancestry I have not.

JULIE. This is my reward for opening my heart to anyone so unworthy, with whom I have talked about my family honor.

JEAN. Dishonor—yes, I said it. I told you not to drink because then one talks too freely and one should never talk.

JULIE. Oh, how I repent all this. If at least you loved me!

JEAN. For the last time—what do you mean? Shall I weep, shall I jump over your riding whip, shall I kiss you, lure you to Lake Como for three weeks, and then—what do you want anyway? This is getting tiresome. But that's the way it always is when you get mixed up in women's affairs. Miss Julie, I see that you are unhappy, I know that you suffer, but I can't understand you. Among my kind there is no nonsense of this sort; we love as we play when work gives us time. We haven't the whole day and night for it like you.

JULIE. You must be good to me and speak to me as though I were a human being.

JEAN. Be one yourself. You spit on me and expect me to stand it.

JULIE. Help me, help me. Only tell me what to do—show me a way out of this!

JEAN. In heaven's name, if I only knew myself.

JULIE. I have been raving, I have been mad, but is there no means of deliverance?

JEAN. Stay here at home and say nothing. No one knows.

JULIE. Impossible. These people know it, and Kristin.

JEAN. They don't know it and could never suspect such a thing.

JULIE [Hesitating]. But—it might happen again.

JEAN. That is true.

JULIE. And the consequences?

JEAN [Frightened]. Consequences—where were my wits not to have thought of that! There is only one thing to do. Get away from here immediately. I can't go with you or they will suspect. You must go alone—away from here—anywhere.

JULIE. Alone? Where? I cannot.

JEAN. You must—and before the Count returns. If you stay, we know how it will be. If one has taken a false step it's likely to happen again as the harm has already been done, and one grows more and more daring until at last all is discovered. Write the Count afterward and confess all—except that it was I. That he could never guess, and I don't think he'll be so anxious to know who it was, anyway.

JULIE. I will go if you'll go with me.

JEAN. Are you raving again? Miss Julie running away with her coachman? All the papers would be full of it and that the Count could never live through.

JULIE. I can't go—I can't stay. Help me, I'm so tired—so weary. Command me, set me in motion—I can't think any more,—can't act—

JEAN. See now, what creatures you aristocrats are! Why do you bristle up and stick up your noses as though you were the lords of creation. Very well—I will command you! Go up and dress yourself and see to it that you have travelling money and then come down. [She hesitates.] Go immediately.

[She still hesitates. He takes her hand and leads her to door.]

JULIE. Speak gently to me, Jean.

JEAN. A command always sounds harsh. Feel it yourself now.

[Exit Julie.]

[Jean draws a sigh of relief, seats himself by the table, takes out a notebook and pencil and counts aloud now and then until, Kristin comes in, dressed for church.]

KRISTIN. My heavens, how it looks here. What's been going on?

JEAN. Oh, Miss Julie dragged in the people. Have you been sleeping so soundly that you didn't hear anything?

KRISTIN. I've slept like a log.

JEAN. And already dressed for church!

KRISTIN. Ye-es, [Sleepily] didn't you promise to go to early service with me?

JEAN. Yes, quite so, and there you have my stock and front. All right.

[He seats himself. Kristin putting on his stock.]

JEAN [Sleepily]. What is the text today?

KRISTIN. St. John's Day! It is of course about the beheading of John the Baptist.

JEAN. I'm afraid it will be terribly long drawn out—that. Hey, you're choking me. I'm so sleepy, so sleepy.

KRISTIN. What have you been doing up all night? You are actually green in the face.

JEAN. I have been sitting here talking to Miss Julie.

KRISTIN. Oh you don't know your place.

[Pause.]

JEAN. Listen, Kristin.

KRISTIN. Well?

JEAN. It's queer about her when you think it over.

KRISTIN. What is queer?

JEAN. The whole thing.

[Pause. Kristin looks at half empty glasses on table.]

KRISTIN. Have you been drinking together, too?

JEAN. Yes!

KRISTIN. For shame. Look me in the eye.

JEAN. Yes.

KRISTIN. Is it possible? Is it possible?

JEAN [After reflecting]. Yes, it is.

KRISTIN. Ugh! That I would never have believed. For shame, for shame!

JEAN. You are not jealous of her?

KRISTIN. No, not of her. But if it had been Clara or Sophie— then I would have scratched your eyes out. So that is what has happened—how I can't understand! No, that wasn't very nice!

JEAN. Are you mad at her?

KRISTIN. No, but with you. That was bad of you, very bad. Poor girl. Do you know what—I don't want to be here in this house any longer where one cannot respect one's betters.

JEAN. Why should one respect them?

KRISTIN. Yes, you can say that, you are so smart. But I don't want to serve people who behave so. It reflects on oneself, I think.

JEAN. Yes, but it's a comfort that they're not a bit better than we.

KRISTIN. No, I don't, think so, for if they are not better there's no use in our trying to better ourselves in this world. And to think of the Count! Think of him who has had so much sorrow all his days? No, I don't want to stay in this house any longer! And to think of it being with such as you! If it had been the Lieutenant—

JEAN. What's that?

KRISTIN. Yes! He was good enough, to be sure, but there's a difference between people just the same. No, this I can never forget. Miss Julie who was always so proud and indifferent to men! One never would believe that she would give herself—and to one like you! She who was ready to have Diana shot because she would run after the gatekeeper's mongrels. Yes, I say it—and here I won't stay any longer and on the twenty-fourth of October I go my way.

JEAN. And then?

KRISTIN. Well, as we've come to talk about it, it's high time you looked around for something else, since we're going to get married.

JEAN. Well, what'll I look for? A married man couldn't get a place like this.

KRISTIN. No, of course not. But you could take a gatekeeper's job or look for it watchman's place in some factory. The government's plums are few, but they are sure. And then the wife and children get a pension—

JEAN [With a grimace]. That's all very fine—all that, but it's not exactly in my line to think about dying for my wife and children just now. I must confess that I have slightly different aspirations.

KRISTIN. Aspirations? Aspirations—anyway you have obligations. Think of those, you.

JEAN. Don't irritate me with talk about my obligations. I know my own business. [He listens.] We'll have plenty of time for all this some other day. Go and get ready and we'll be off to church.

KRISTIN [Listening]. Who's that walking upstairs?

JEAN. I don't know—unless it's Clara.

KRISTIN [Starting to go]. It could never be the Count who has come home without anyone hearing him?

JEAN [Frightened]. The Count! I can't believe that. He would have rung the bell.

KRISTIN. God help us! Never have I been mixed up in anything like this!

[Exit Kristin. The sun has risen and lights up the scene. Presently the sunshine comes in through windows at an angle. Jean goes to door and motions. Enter Julie, dressed for travelling, carrying a small bird cage covered with a cloth, which she places on a chair.]

JULIE. I am ready!

JEAN. Hush, Kristin is stirring!

[Julie frightened and nervous throughout following scene.]

JULIE. Does she suspect anything?

JEAN. She knows nothing. But, good heavens, how you look!

JULIE. Why?

JEAN. You are pale as a ghost.

JULIE [Sighs]. Am I? Oh, the sun is rising, the sun!

JEAN. And now the troll's spell is broken.

JULIE. The trolls have indeed been at work this night. But, Jean, listen—come with me, I have money enough.

JEAN. Plenty?

JULIE. Enough to start with. Go with me for I can't go alone—today, midsummer day. Think of the stuffy train, packed in with the crowds of people staring at one; the long stops at the stations when one would be speeding away. No, I cannot, I cannot! And then the memories, childhood's memories of midsummer day—the church decorated with birch branches and syringa blossoms; the festive dinner table with relations and friends, afternoon in the park, music, dancing, flowers and games—oh, one may fly, fly, but anguish and remorse follow in the pack wagon.

JEAN. I'll go with you—if we leave instantly—before it's too late.

JULIE. Go and dress then. [She takes up bird cage.]

JEAN. But no baggage! That would betray us.

JULIE. Nothing but what we can take in the coupe.

[Jean has picked up his hat.]

JEAN. What have you there?

JULIE. It's only my canary. I cannot, will not, leave it behind.

JEAN. So we are to lug a bird cage with us. Are you crazy? Let go of it.

JULIE. It is all I take from home. The only living creature that cares for me. Don't be hard—let me take it with me.

JEAN. Let go the cage and don't talk so loud. Kristin will hear us.

JULIE. No, I will not leave it to strange hands. I would rather see it dead.

JEAN. Give me the creature. I'll fix it.

JULIE. Yes, but don't hurt it. Don't—no, I cannot.

JEAN. Let go. I can.

JULIE [Takes the canary from cage]. Oh, my little siren. Must your mistress part with you?

JEAN. Be so good as not to make a scene. Your welfare, your life, is at stake. So—quickly. [Snatches bird from her and goes to chopping block and takes up meat chopper]. You should have learned how to chop off a chicken's head instead of shooting with a revolver. [He chops off the bird's head]. Then you wouldn't swoon at a drop of blood.

JULIE [Shrieks]. Kill me, too. Kill me! You who can butcher an innocent bird without a tremble. Oh, how I shrink from you. I curse the moment I first saw you. I curse the moment I was conceived in my mother's womb.

JEAN. Come now! What good is your cursing, let's be off.

JULIE [Looks toward chopping block as though obsessed by thought of the slain bird]. No, I cannot. I must see—hush, a carriage is passing. Don't you think I can stand the sight of blood? You think I am weak. Oh, I should like to see your blood flowing— to see your brain on the chopping block, all your sex swimming in a sea of blood. I believe I could drink out of your skull, bathe my feet in your breast and eat your heart cooked whole. You think I am weak; you believe that I love you because my life has mingled with yours; you think that I would carry your offspring under my heart, and nourish it with my blood—give birth to your child and take your name! Hear, you, what are you called, what is your family name? But I'm sure you have none. I should be "Mrs. Gate-Keeper," perhaps, or "Madame Dumpheap." You dog with my collar on, you lackey with my father's hallmark on your buttons. I play rival to my cook—oh—oh—oh! You believe that I am cowardly and want to run away. No, now I shall stay. The thunder may roll. My father will return—and find his desk broken into—his money gone! Then he will ring—that bell. A scuffle with his servant—then sends for the police—and then I tell all—everything! Oh, it will be beautiful to have it all over with—if only that were the end! And my father—he'll have a shock and die, and then that will be the end. Then they will place his swords across the coffin—and the Count's line is extinct. The serf's line will continue in an orphanage, win honors in the gutter and end in prison.

JEAN. Now it is the king's blood talking. Splendid, Miss Julie! Only keep the miller in his sack.

[Enter Kristin with prayer-book in hand.]

JULIE [Hastening to Kristin and falls in her arms as though seeking protection]. Help me, Kristin, help me against this man.

KRISTIN [Cold and unmoved]. What kind of performance is this for a holy day morning? What does this mean—this noise and fuss?

JULIE. Kristin, you are a woman,—and my friend. Beware of this wretch.

JEAN [A little embarrassed and surprised]. While the ladies are arguing I'll go and shave myself.

[Jean goes, R.]

JULIE. You must understand me—you must listen to me.

KRISTIN. No—I can't understand all this bosh. Where may you be going in your traveling dress?—and he had his hat on! Hey?

JULIE. Listen to me, Kristin, listen to me and I'll tell you everything.

KRISTIN. I don't want to know anything—

JULIE. You must listen to me—

KRISTIN. What about? Is it that foolishness with Jean? That doesn't concern me at all. That I won't be mixed up with, but if you're trying to lure him to run away with you then we must put a stop to it.

JULIE [Nervously]. Try to be calm now Kristin, and listen to me. I can't stay here and Jean can't stay here. That being true, we must leave—Kristin.

KRISTIN. Hm, hm!

JULIE [Brightening up]. But I have an idea—what if we three should go—away—to foreign parts. To Switzerland and set up a hotel together—I have money you see—and Jean and I would back the whole thing, you could run the kitchen. Won't that be fine? Say yes, now—and come with us—there everything would be arranged—say yes! [Throws her arms around Kristin and coaxes her].

KRISTIN [Cold and reflecting]. Hm—hm!

JULIE [Presto tempo]. You leave never been out and traveled, Kristin. You shall look about you in the world. Yon can't believe how pleasant traveling on a train is—new faces continually, new countries—and we'll go to Hamburg—and passing through we'll see the zoological gardens—that you will like—then we'll go to the theatre and hear the opera—and when we reach Munich there will be the museum—there are Rubins and Raphaels and all the big painters that you know—you have heard of Munich—where King Ludwig lived—the King, you know, who went mad. Then we'll see his palace—a palace like those in the Sagas—and from there it isn't far to Switzerland—and the Alps, the Alps mind you with snow in mid-summer. And there oranges grow and laurel—green all the year round if—[Jean is seen in the doorway R. stropping his razor on the strop which he holds between his teeth and left hand. He listens and nods his head favorably now and then. Julie continues, tempo prestissimo] And there we'll take a hotel and I'll sit taking the cash while Jean greets the guests—goes out and markets writes letters—that will be life, you may believe—then the train whistles—then the omnibus comes—then a bell rings upstairs, then in the restaurant—and then I make out the bills—and I can salt them—you can't think how people tremble when they receive their bill—and you—you can sit like a lady—of course you won't have to stand over the stove—you can dress finely and neatly when you show yourself to the people—and you with your appearance—

Oh, I'm not flattering, you can catch a husband some fine day—a rich Englishman perhaps—they are so easy to—[Slowing up] to catch—Then we'll be rich—and then we'll build a villa by Lake Como—to be sure it rains sometimes—but [becoming languid] the sun must shine too sometimes——although it seems dark——and if not—we can at least travel homeward—and come back—here—or some other place.

KRISTIN. Listen now. Does Miss Julie believe in all this?

[Julie going to pieces.]

JULIE. Do I believe in it?

KRISTIN. Yes.

JULIE [Tired]. I don't know. I don't believe in anything any more. [Sinks down on bench, and takes head in her hand on table.] In nothing—nothing!

KRISTIN [Turns to R. and looks toward Jean]. So—you intended to run away?

JEAN [Rather shamefaced comes forward and puts razor on table]. Run away? That's putting it rather strong. You heard Miss Julie's project, I think it might be carried out.

KRISTIN. Now listen to that! Was it meant that I should be her cook—

JEAN [Sharply]. Be so good as to use proper language when you speak of your mistress.

KRISTIN. Mistress?

JEAN. Yes.

KRISTIN. No—hear! Listen to him!

JEAN. Yes, you listen—you need to, and talk less. Miss Julie is your mistress and for the same reason that you do not respect her now you should not respect yourself.

KRISTIN. I have always had so much respect for myself—

JEAN. That you never had any left for others!

KRISTIN. I have never lowered my position. Let any one say, if they can, that the Count's cook has had anything to do with the riding master or the swineherd. Let them come and say it!

JEAN. Yes, you happened to get a fine fellow. That was your good luck.

KRISTIN. Yes, a fine fellow—who sells the Count's oats from his stable.

JEAN. Is it for you to say anything—you who get a commission on all the groceries and a bribe from the butcher?

KRISTIN. What's that?

JEAN. And you can't have respect for your master and mistress any longer—you, you!

KRISTIN [Glad to change the subject]. Are you coming to church with me? You need a good sermon for your actions.

JEAN. No, I'm not going to church today. You can go alone—and confess your doings.

KRISTIN. Yes, that I shall do, and I shall return with so much forgiveness that there will be enough for you too. The Savior suffered and died on the cross for all our sins, and when we go to Him in faith and a repentant spirit he takes our sins on Himself.

JULIE. Do you believe that, Kristin?

KRISTIN. That is my life's belief, as true as I stand here. And that was my childhood's belief that I have kept since my youth, Miss Julie. And where sin overflows, there mercy overflows also.

JULIE. Oh, if I only had your faith. Oh, if—

KRISTIN. Yes, but you see that is not given without God's particular grace, and that is not allotted to all, that!

JULIE. Who are the chosen?

KRISTIN. That is the great secret of the Kingdom of Grace, and the Lord has no respect for persons. But there the last shall be first.

JULIE. But then has he respect for the last—the lowliest person?

KRISTIN [Continuing]. It is easier for a camel to pass through the eye of a needle than for a rich man to enter the Kingdom of Heaven. That's the way it is, Miss Julie. However—now I am going—alone. And on any way I shall stop in and tell the stable boy not to let any horses go out in case any one wants to get away before the Count comes home. Good bye.

[Exit Kristin.]

JEAN. Such a devil. And all this on account of your confounded canary!

JULIE [Tired]. Oh, don't speak of the canary—do you see any way out—any end to this?

JEAN [Thinking]. No.

JULIE. What would you do in my place?

JEAN. In your place—wait. As a noble lady, as a woman—fallen— I don't know. Yes, now I know.

JULIE [She takes up razor from table and makes gestures saying] This?

JEAN. Yes. But I should not do it, mark you, for there is a difference between us.

JULIE. Because you are a man and I am a woman? What other difference is there?

JEAN. That very difference—of man and woman.

JULIE [Razor in hand]. I want to do it—but I can't. My father couldn't either that time when he should have done it.

JEAN. No, he was right, not to do it—he had to avenge himself first.

119

JULIE. And now my mother revenges herself again through me.

JEAN. Haven't you loved your father, Miss Julie?

JULIE. Yes, deeply. But I have probably hated him too, I must have—without being aware of it. And it is due to my father's training that I have learned to scorn my own sex. Between them both they have made me half man, half woman. Whose is the fault for what has happened—my father's? My mother's? My own? I haven't anything of my own. I haven't a thought which was not nay father's—not a passion that wasn't my mother's. And last of all from my betrothed the idea that all people are equal. For that I now call him a wretch. How can it be my own fault then? Throw the burden on Jesus as Kristin did? No, I am too proud, too intelligent, thanks to my father's teaching.—And that a rich man cannot enter the Kingdom of Heaven—that is a lie, and Kristin, who has money in the savings bank—she surely cannot enter there. Whose is the fault? What does it concern us whose fault it is? It is I who must bear the burden and the consequences.

JEAN. Yes, but—

[Two sharp rings on bell are heard. Julie starts to her feet.
Jean changes his coat.]

JEAN. The Count—has returned. Think if Kristin has—[Goes up to speaking tube and listens.]

JULIE. Now he has seen the desk!

JEAN [Speaking in the tube]. It is Jean, Excellency. [Listens]. Yes, Excellency. [Listens].Yes, Excellency,—right away—immediately, Excellency. Yes—in half an hour.

JULIE [In great agitation]. What did he say? In Heaven's name, what did he say?

JEAN. He wants his boots and coffee in a half hour.

JULIE. In half an hour then. Oh, I'm so tired—I'm incapable of feeling, not able to be sorry, not able to go, not able to stay, not able to live—not able to die. Help me now. Command me—I will obey like a dog. Do me this last service save my honor. Save his name. You know what I have the will to do—but cannot do. You will it and command me to execute your will.

JEAN. I don't know why—but now I can't either.—I don't understand myself. It is absolutely as though this coat does it—but I can't command you now. And since the Count spoke to me—I can't account for it—but oh, it is that damned servant in my back—I believe if the Count came in here now and told me to cut my throat I would do it on the spot.

JULIE. Make believe you are he—and I you. You could act so well a little while ago when you knelt at my feet. Then you were a nobleman—or haven't you ever been at the theatre and seen the hypnotist—[Jean nods] He says to his subject "Take the broom," and he takes it; he says, "Sweep," and he sweeps.

JEAN. Then the subject must be asleep!

JULIE [Ecstatically]. I sleep already. The whole room is like smoke before me—and you are like a tall black stove, like a man clad in black clothes with a high hat; and your eyes gleam like the hot coals when the fire is dying; and your face a white spot like fallen ashes. [The sunshine is coming in through the windows and falls on Jean. Julie rubs her hands as though warming them before a fire]. It is so warm and good—and so bright and quiet!

JEAN [Takes razor and puts it in her hand]. There is the broom, go now while it's bright—out to the hay loft—and—[He whispers in her ear.]

JULIE [Rousing herself]. Thanks. And now I go to rest. But tell me this—the foremost may receive the gift of Grace? Say it, even if you don't believe it.

JEAN. The foremost? No, I can't say that. But wait, Miss Julie—you are no longer among the foremost since you are of the lowliest.

JULIE. That's true, I am the lowliest—the lowliest of the lowly. Oh, now I can't go. Tell me once more that I must go.

JEAN. No, now I cannot either—I cannot.

JULIE. And the first shall be last——

JEAN. Don't think. You take my strength from me, too, so that I become cowardly.—What—I thought I heard the bell!—No! To be afraid of the sound of is bell! But it's not the bell—it's someone behind the bell, the hand that sets the lull in motion—and something else that sets the land in motion. But stop your cars, stop your ears. Then he will only ring louder and keep on ringing until it's answered—and then it is too late! Then come the police and then—[Two loud rings on bell are heard, Jean falls in a heap for a moment, but straightens up immediately.] It is horrible! But there is no other way. Go!

[Countess Julie goes out resolutely.]

CURTAIN.

THE OUTLAW

CHARACTERS
> THORFINN, Erl of Iceland
> VALGERD, his wife
> GUNLOED, their daughter
> GUNNAR, a Crusader
> ORM, a minstrel, foster brother to Thorfinn
> A THRALL
> A MESSENGER

Action takes place in Iceland.

[SCENE—A hut, door at back, window-holes, right and, left, closed by big heavy wooden shutters. Wooden benches against walls, the high bench, a sort of rude throne, at left. The uprights of this high beach are carved with images of the gods Odin and Thor. From the wall beams hang swords, battle axes and shields. Near the high bench stands a harp. Gunloed stands at an open window-hole peering out; through the opening one gets a glimpse of the sea lighted by the aurora borealis. Valgerd sits by the fire, which is in the middle of the room, spinning.]

VALGERD. Close the window-hole.

[Gunloed is silent.]

VALGERD. Gunloed!

GUNLOED. Did you speak, mother?

VALGERD. What are you doing?

GUNLOED. I am watching the sea.

VALGERD. When will you learn to forget?

GUNLOED. Take everything away from me but memories!

VALGERD. Look forward—not back.

GUNLOED. Who reproaches the strong viking who looks back when he is quitting his native strand?

VALGERD. You have had three winters to make your farewell.

GUNLOED. You speak truly—three winters! For here never came a summer!

VALGERD. When the floating ice melts, then shall spring be here.

GUNLOED. The Northern Lights melt no ice.

VALGERD. Nor your tears.

GUNLOED. You never saw me weep.

VALGERD. But I have heard you. As long as you do that, you are a child.

GUNLOED. I am not a child.

VALGERD. If you would be a woman, suffer in silence.

GUNLOED. I'll cast sorrow from me, mother.

VALGERD. No, no—bury it, as your deepest treasure. The seed must not lie on top of the earth if it would sprout and ripen. You have a deep sorrow. It should bear great gladness—and great peace.

GUNLOED [After a pause]. I shall forget.

VALGERD. Everything?

GUNLOED. I shall try.

VALGERD. Can you forget your father's hardness?

GUNLOED. That I have forgotten.

VALGERD. Can you forget that there was a time when your fore-fathers' dwelling stood on Broevikens' strand? Where the south wind sang in the oak wood when the ice-bound seas ran free—where the hemlocks gave forth their fragrance and the finches twittered among the linden trees—and Balder, the God of spring and joy, lulled you to sleep on the green meadows? Can you forget all this, while you listen to the sea gulls' plaints on these bare rocks and cliffs, and the cold storms out of the north howl through the stunted birches?

GUNLOED. Yes!

VALGERD. Can you forget the friend of your childhood from whom your father tore you to save you from the white Christ?

GUNLOED [in desperation]. Yes, yes!

VALGERD. You are weeping.

GUNLOED [Disturbed]. Some one is walking out there. Perhaps father is coming home.

VALGERD. Will you bear in mind every day without tears that we now dwell in the land of ice—fugitives from the kingdom of Svea and hated here by the Christ-men? But we have suffered no loss of greatness, although we have not been baptized and kissed the bishop's hand. Have you ever spoken to any of the Christians since we have been here?

GUNLOED [After a pause]. No. Tell me, mother, is it true that father is to be Erl here in Iceland, too?

VALGERD. Don't let that trouble you, child.

GUNLOED. Then I'm afraid he will fare badly with the Christians.

VALGERD. You fear that?

GUNLOED. Some one is out there.

VALGERD [Anxiously]. Did you see the ship lying in the inlet this morning?

GUNLOED. With heart-felt gladness!

VALGERD. Bore it the figure-head of Thorfinn?

GUNLOED. That I could not make out.

VALGERD. Have a care, girl.

GUNLOED. Is it tonight that I may go out?

VALGERD. Tomorrow—that you know well.

GUNLOED Mother!

VALGERD [Going]. Mind the fire. [Valgerd goes.]

[Gunloed looks after her mother, then cautiously takes from her breast a crucifix, puts it on the high bench and falls on her knees.]

GUNLOED. Christ, Christ, forgive me the lie I told. [Springs up noticing the images of the gods on the high bench.] No, I cannot pray before these wicked images. [She looks for another place.] Holy St. Olof, holy—oh, I can't remember how the bishop named her! God! God! Cast me not into purgatory for this sin! I will repeat the whole long prayer of the monks—credo, credo—in patrem—oh, I have forgotten that too. I shall give five tall candles for the altar of the mother of God the next time I go to the chapel—Credo, in patrem omnipotentem—[Kissing the crucifix eagerly.]

[A song is heard outside the hut accompanied by a lyre.]

A crusader went out to the Holy Land,
O, Christ, take the maiden's soul in hand,
And to your kingdom bring her!
I'll return, mayhap, when the spruce trees bloom.

Summers three he wanders far from thee,
Where nightingales sing their delight,
And masses he holds both day and night,
At the holy sepulchre's chapel.
I'll return, mayhap, when the spruce trees bloom.

When the palm trees bud on Jordan's strand,
Then makes he a prayer to God,
That he may return to his native land,
And press to his heart his love.
I'll return, my love, when the spruce trees bloom.

GUNLOED [At beginning of song springs up and then listens with more and more agitation and eagerness. When the song is over she goes toward door to bolt it, but so slowly that Gunnar is able to enter before she slips the bolt. Gunnar is clad in the costume of a crusader with a lyre swung across his shoulder.]

GUNNAR. Gunloed! [They embrace. Gunloed pulls away and goes toward door.] You are afraid of me? What is it, Gunloed?

GUNLOED. You never took me in your arms before!

GUNNAR. We were children then!

GUNLOED You are right—we were children then. What means that silver falcon on your shield? I saw it on your ship's bow this morning, too.

GUNNAR. You saw my ship—you knew my song, and you would have barred the door against me! What am I to understand, Gunloed?

GUNLOED. Oh, ask me nothing! I am so unquiet of spirit but sit and let me talk to you.

GUNNAR [Sits]. You are silent.

GUNLOED. You are silent, too.

GUNNAR [Pulls her to his side]. Gunloed, Gunloed—has the snow fallen so heavily that memories have been chilled even the mountains here burst forth with fire—and you are cold as a snow wind—but speak—speak! Why are you here in Iceland—and what has happened?

GUNLOED. Terrible things—and more may follow if you stay here longer.—[Springs up]. Go, before my father comes.

GUNNAR. Do you think I would leave you now—I, who have sought you for long years? When I could not find you in the home land I went to the wars against the Saracens to seek you the other side of the grave. But my time had not yet come; when the fourth spring came, I heard through wandering merchants that you were to be found here. Now I have found you—and you wish me to leave you in this heathen darkness.

GUNLOED. I am not alone!

GUNNAR. Your father does not love you—your mother does not understand you, and they are both heathen.

GUNLOED. I have friends among the Christians.

GUNNAR. Then you have become a Christian, Gunloed!—the holy virgin has heard my prayer.

GUNLOED. Yes, yes! Oh, let me kiss the cross you bear on your shoulder—that you got at the holy sepulchre!

GUNNAR. Now I give you a brother Christian's kiss—the first, Gunloed, you have from me.

GUNLOED. You must never kiss me again.

GUNNAR. But tell me, how did you become a Christian?

GUNLOED. First I believed in my father—he was so strong; then I believed in my mother—she was so good; last I believed in you— you were so strong and good—and so beautiful; and when you went away—I stood alone—myself I could never believe in—I was so weak; then I thought of your God, whom you so often begged me to love—and I prayed to Him.

GUNNAR. And the old gods—

GUNLOED. I have never been able to believe in them—although my father commanded me to do so—they are wicked.

GUNNAR. Who has taught you to pray? Who gave you the crucifix?

GUNLOED. The bishop.

GUNNAR. And that no one knows?

GUNLOED. No—I have had to lie to my mother and that troubles me.

GUNNAR. And your father hid you here so that the Christians should not get you?

GUNLOED. Yes—and now he is expected home from Norway with followers as he is to be Erl of the island.

GUNNAR. God forbid!

GUNLOED. Yes—yes—but you must not delay. He is expected home tonight.

GUNNAR. Good—there beyond Hjaerleif's headland lies my ship.—Out to sea! There is a land wind, and before the first cock's crow we shall be beyond pursuit.

GUNLOED. Yes! Yes!

GUNNAR. Soon we should be at Ostergoetland—where the summer is still green—and there you shall live in my castle which I have built where your father's house stood.

GUNLOED. Does not that still stand?

GUNNAR. No—it was burned.

GUNLOED. By the Christians?

GUNNAR. You are so passionate, Gunloed!

GUNLOED. I suffer to say I would rather be a heathen.

GUNNAR. What are you saying, girl!

GUNLOED. [After a pause]. Forgive me, forgive me—I am in such a wild mood—and when I see the Christians, who should be examples, commit such deeds—

GUNNAR. Crush out that thought, Gunloed—it is ungodly. Do you see this wreath?

GUNLOED. Where did you gather it?

GUNNAR. You recognize the flowers, Gunloed?

GUNLOED. They grew in my father's garden—may I keep them?

GUNNAR. Gladly—but, why do you care to have them when we are going to journey there ourselves?

GUNLOED. I shall look at them the long winter through—the hemlock shall remind me of the green woods and the anemones of the blue sky.

GUNNAR. And when they are withered—

GUNLOED. Of that I do not think.

GUNNAR. Then go with me from this drear land—far away, and there where our childhood was spent we will live as free as the birds among the flowers and sunshine. There you shall not go in stealth to the temple of the Lord when the bells tell you of the Sabbath. Oh, you shall see the new chapel with its vaulted roof and high pillared aisles. And hear the acolytes singing when the bishop lights the incense on the high altar. There shall you solemnize the God service with those of Christ and you shall feel you heart cleansed of sin.

GUNLOED. Shall I fly—leave my mother?

GUNNAR. She will forgive you some time.

GUNLOED. But my father would call me cowardly and that I would never allow.

GUNNAR. That you must endure for the sake of your belief.

GUNLOED. Thorfinn's daughter was never cowardly.

GUNNAR. Your father does not love you, and he will hate you when he knows of your conversion.

GUNLOED. That he may do—but he shall never despise me.

GUNNAR. You surrender your love, Gunloed.

GUNLOED. Love!—I remember—there was a maiden—she had a friend who went away—after, she was never again glad—she only sat sewing silk and gold—what she was making no one knew—and when they asked her she would only weep. And when they asked her why she wept, she never answered—only wept. She grew pale of cheek and her mother made ready her shroud.—Then there came an old woman and she said it was love. Gunnar,—I never wept when you went away as father says it is weak to shed tears; I never sewed silk and gold for that my mother has never taught me to do—then had I not love?

GUNNAR. You have often thought of me during these years?

GUNLOED. I have dreamed so often of you, and this morning when I stood by the window where I linger so willingly and, gazing over the sea, I saw your ship come up out of the east, I became unquiet although I did not know it was your ship.

GUNNAR. Why do you gaze so willingly over the sea?

GUNLOED. You ask many questions!

GUNNAR. Why did you want to close the door against me?

GUNLOED. [Silent].

GUNNAR. Why didn't you close it?

GUNLOED. [Silent].

GUNNAR. Why are you silent?

[Gunloed bursts into tears.]

GUNNAR. You weep, Gunloed, and you know why? I know,—you love! [Takes her in his arms and kisses her.]

GUNLOED. [Tearing herself away]. You must not kiss me! Go!

GUNNAR. Yes—and you shall go with me.

GUNLOED. I do not care to be commanded by you—and I shall not obey.

GUNNAR. The volcano gives forth fire—and burns itself out!

GUNLOED. You have destroyed my peace—forever! Go and let me forget you.

GUNNAR. Do you know what the silver falcon with the ribbon stands for? It is the symbol of the wild girl I shall tame.

GUNLOED. [With force]. You! Go before I hate you!—No one yet has bent my will!

GUNNAR. The wild fire of the viking's blood still burns in your veins, but it shall be quenched. A day and a night shall I wait for you. And you will come—mild as a dove seeking shelter, although you now would fly above the clouds like a wild falcon. But I still hold the ribbon in my hand—that is your love, which you cannot tear away. When twilight falls again you will come. Till then, farewell. [Goes to the door and stops.]

GUNLOED. [Silent.]

GUNNAR. [Going.] Farewell.

GUNLOED. We shall see, proud knight, who comes first. When this garland shall bloom again, then shall I come. [Throws garland in fire. She watches it burn in a thoughtful mood. When it is quite burnt she breaks into tears again and falls on her knees.] God! God! Soften my proud spirit! Oh, that he should leave me! [Hastens to door. At same moment Valgerd enters, passes Gunloed, and goes to fire.]

VALGERD. Why did you not tend the fire?

GUNLOED. [Silent.]

VALGERD [Putting her hand against Gunloed's heart]. You have a secret!

GUNLOED. Yes, mother, yes.

VALGERD. Hide it well.

GUNLOED. Oh, I must speak—I can't bear it any longer.

VALGERD. When saw you a mother who did not know a daughter's secrets?

GUNLOED. Who told you mine?

VALGERD [Harshly]. Dry your tears.

[A pause.]

GUNLOED. Oh, let me go out—on the mountains—on the strand. It is so stifling here.

VALGERD. Go up to the loft—and you can be alone. [Enter a thrall.] What would you?

THRALL. The Erl's trumpets are heard beyond the rocks and the storm is growing.

VALGERD. Has darkness fallen?

THRALL. Yes, and a terrible darkness it is.

[A pause.]

GUNLOED. Send out a boat—two—as many as can be found.

THRALL. All the boats are out for the hunt.

GUNLOED. Light beacon fires.

THRALL. All the fuel is so rain-soaked that we haven't had so much as a twig on the hearth all the evening.

VALGERD. Away!

THRALL. How will it go with the Erl?

VALGERD. Does that concern you?

[Thrall goes.]

GUNLOED. You have not forgotten your wrong!

VALGERD. Nor my revenge! One should not lay hands on the daughter of an Erl!

GUNLOED. So be it. Now your moment has come—take your revenge—I'll show you how—like this. [Takes a lighted torch.] Put this torch in the window-hole on the right and you wreck him. Put it in the left and you save him—

VALGERD [Interrupts]. Give me the torch and leave me.

GUNLOED. There is a sacrifice which can pacify your god's. Sacrifice your revenge.

VALGERD. [Takes torch, hesitates, and goes quickly to left window-hole and places it there. Trumpets are heard]. You struck me, Thorfinn—I swore revenge—I shall humble you with a kind deed.

GUNLOED [Unseen by Valgerd has entered and falls on her mother's neck]. Thanks, mother.

VALGERD [Disconcerted]. Haven't you gone—

GUNLOED. Now I shall go. [Gunloed goes.]

VALGERD [Alone by the window-hole]. You shout for help, you mighty man, who always helped yourself. [Trumpets are heard.] Where is now your might—where is your kingdom—[A gust of wind blows out the lighted torch. Valgerd, terribly frightened, takes torch and lights it.] Oh, he will perish! What shall I do? Pray? To whom? Odin? Njard? Ogir? I have called to them for four times ten years, but never have they answered. I have sacrificed, but never have they helped. Thou, God, however you may be called—Thou mighty one, who bids the sun to rise and set, thou tremendous one who rules over the winds and water—to you will I pray, to you will I sacrifice my revenge if you will save him.

[Orm enters unnoticed.]

ORM. Good evening to you, Valgerd. Put on your cloak—the wind is sharp.

VALGERD [Disconcerted, takes down torch and closes window-hole.] Welcome, Orm.

ORM. Thanks.

VALGERD. How is it with you, Orm?

ORM. Tolerable enough—when one gets near the big logs.

VALGERD [Irritated]. How went the journey I mean?

ORM. That is a long saga.

VALGERD. Make it short.

ORM. Well, as you know, we fared to Norway, seeking men and timber.

VALGERD. Orm!

ORM. Valgerd!

VALGERD. You have not spoken a word of the Erl.

ORM. Have you asked a word about your mate?

VALGERD. Where is he? Lives he?

ORM. I know not.

VALGERD. You know not!—you, his foster brother? Where did you part from him?

ORM. Far out in the gulf. It was merry out there you may believe. You should have seen him swimming with my lyre in his hand. The sea-weed was so tangled in his beard and hair that one was tempted to believe that it was Neptune himself. Just then came a wave as big as a house—

VALGERD. And then?

ORM. And then—I saw my lyre no more.

VALGERD. Orm! You jest while your lord and brother is perhaps perishing out there! I command you—go at once and seek him! Do you hear?

ORM. Why, what is the matter? You were never before so concerned about your mate! You might find time to give me a drink of ale before I go.

VALGERD. Warm your knees by the hearth. I shall go—and defy wind and storm.

ORM. [Taking her hounds]. Woman, woman—after all, you are a woman!

VALGERD [Angry]. Let go my hand.

ORM. Now the Erl is saved!

VALGERD. Saved?

ORM. Yes, you have been given back to him—and that is his voice now. [Goes.]

> [Voices of Thorfinn and Orm are heard outside,
> Thorfinn laughing loudly.]

VALGERD. The Erl comes—he laughs—that I have never heard before—oh, there is something terrible approaching! [Wrings her hands.]

> [Enter Thorfinn and Orm.]

THORFINN [Laughing]. That was a murderous sight—

ORM. Yes, I promise you!

VALGERD. Welcome home, mate.

THORFINN. Thanks, wife. Have you been out in the rain? Your eyes are wet.

VALGERD. You are so merry!

THORFINN. Merry? Yes—yes.

VALGERD. What became of your ships?

ORM. They went to the bottom—all but one.

VALGERD [To Thorfinn]. And you can nevertheless be so gay?

THORFINN. Ho! Ho! Timber grows in plenty in the north!

ORM. Now perhaps we might have something life-giving.

THORFINN. Well said! Fetch some ale, wife, and let's be merry.

ORM. And we'll thank the gods who saved us.

THORFINN. When will you ever outgrow those sagas, Orm?

ORM. Why do you force your wife and daughter to believe in them?

THORFINN. Women folk should have gods.

ORM. Whom do you believe helped you out there in the storm?

THORFINN. I helped myself.

ORM. And yet you cried out to Ake-Thor when the big wave swallowed you.

THORFINN. There you lie.

ORM. Orm never lies.

THORFINN. Orm is a poet!

ORM. Thorfinn must have swallowed too much sea water when he cried for help to have such a bitter tongue.

THORFINN. Take care of your own tongue, Orm.

[Valgerd with drinking horns.]

VALGERD. Here, foster brothers, I drink to your oath of friendship and better luck for your next voyage.

THORFINN. I forbid you to speak of that again. [They drink. Thorfinn takes horn hastily from mouth and asks] Where is the child?

VALGERD [Troubled]. She is in the loft.

THORFINN. Call her hither.

VALGERD. She's not well.

THORFINN [Looks sharply at Valgerd]. She shall—come!

VALGERD. You don't mean that.

THORFINN. Did you hear the word?

VALGERD. It is not your last.

THORFINN. A man has but one, though woman must always have the last.

VALGERD [Weakly]. You mock me.

THORFINN. You are angry I believe.

VALGERD. You laugh so much tonight.

[Goes out.]

THORFINN. Orm! A thought comes to me.

ORM. If it's a great one you had better hide it. Great thoughts are scarce these days.

THORFINN. Did you notice my wife?

ORM. I never notice other men's wives.

THORFINN. How kindly and mild she was.

ORM. She pitied you.

THORFINN. Pitied me?

ORM. Yes, because sorrow that laughs is the laughter of death, she thought.

THORFINN. Woman cannot think.

ORM. No, not with her head, but with her heart. That's why she has a smaller head but a bigger breast than we.

THORFINN. Forebodings of evil torture me.

ORM. Poor Thorfinn.

THORFINN. My child! Orm! When she comes do you bid her drink from the horn to Asa-Odin.

ORM. The fox scents against, the wind. I understand.

THORFINN. Be ready—they come.

ORM. Be not hard with the child, Thorfinn, or you will have me to reckon with.

[Valgerd and Gunloed enter. The latter heavy with sleepiness.]

GUNLOED. Welcome home, father.

THORFINN. Do you speak truthfully?

GUNLOED. [Silent.]

THORFINN. You are ill, are you not?

GUNLOED. I am not quite myself.

THORFINN. I fear so.

ORM [Waning a drinking horn over the fire]. Come, Gunloed, and empty this sacred horn to Odin who saved your father from shipwreck.

[All empty their horns except Gunloed.]

THORFINN [Tremblingly]. Drink, Gunloed.

[Gunloed throws the horn on floor and goes to Thorfinn and buries her head in his lap.]

GUNLOED. Hear me, father. I am a Christian. Do with me what you will—my soul you cannot destroy. God and the Saints will protect it.

[Thorfinn is beside himself with grief and rage. Rises and pushes Gunloed away from him and tries to speak, but words fail him. Sits on his high bench again in silence. Orm goes to the women and speaks quietly to them. They go toward door. Suddenly Gunloed turns.]

GUNLOED. No! I won't go. I must speak that you, my father, may not go to the grave with a lie—for your whole life has been a lie! I shall sacrifice the child's respect—love I have never felt—and prove to you what terrible guilt you have gathered on your head. Know then, you have taught me to hate—for when did you ever give me love—you taught me to fear the great Erl Thorfinn and you have succeeded, because I tremble before your harshness. I respect your many scars and great deeds, but you never taught me to love my father. You always thrust me away when I wanted to come to you—you poisoned my soul and now you see God's punishment. You have made me a criminal—for such I am at this moment, but it cannot be otherwise. Why do you hate my belief? Because it is love and yours is hate! Oh, father, father, I want to kiss the clouds from your brow. I wanted to caress your white locks and make you forget the sorrows that whitened them. I wanted to support you when your steps began to falter—Oh! forget what I have said—open your arms [falls on her knees] and take me to your heart. Look at me tenderly—just once before it is too late. Speak one word—[springs to her feet] Oh, your glance freezes me! You will not! I shall pray for power to love you. [Bursts into tears and goes out, followed by Valgerd, Orm goes forward to Thorfinn.]

THORFINN. Sing for me, Orm.

ORM. Orm sings nothing but lies.

THORFINN. Lie then.

ORM. Was the truth so bitter?

THORFINN. What do you say?

ORM. Never mind. You shall hear more from me later.

THORFINN. Orm, you are my friend!

ORM. H'm—of course!

THORFINN. I lack peace.

ORM. There are two ways to gain peace: one is never to do anything one regrets—the other never to regret anything one does!

THORFINN. But if one has already done what one regrets?

ORM. Thorfinn! That is to say, you regret your harshness toward your child?

THORFINN [Angry]. I regret nothing. And as far as the child is concerned you had better hold your tongue!

ORM. Hear you, Thorfinn—have you ever thought about what your life has been?

THORFINN. Thinking is for old women—doing has been my life.

ORM. What do you intend to do now?

THORFINN. What do I intend to do now?

ORM. Yes.

THORFINN [Shaken, is silent.]

ORM. You see how even a little thought struck you—think then if a big thought should come. Why don't you dare to look back? Because you are afraid of the sights you would see.

THORFINN. Let the past remain buried.

ORM. No, I shall tear the corpses from their graves and they shall stare at you with their empty orbits until you quake with anguish and fear—and you shall see that with all your strength you were not a man.

THORFINN. What are you saying, madman?

ORM. Yes, shout—you are still a boy. Yes, you—I have seen big, tall children with bushy beards and gray hairs and crooked backs as well.

THORFINN. Hold your tongue, Orm.

ORM. Shout until the hut trembles—the truth you cannot shout down.

THORFINN. Silence, before I strike you!

ORM. Strike! Strike me to death—tear the tongue out of my mouth—with copper trumpets shall the truth be blasted into your ears, "Your life has been a lie."

THORFINN [With repressed anger and pain]. Orm, I beg of you—speak no more.

ORM. Yes, Thorfinn, I shall speak. Feel how the earth trembles under you. That means an earthquake! The whole earth trembles these days, for she is about to give birth. She is to bring forth in dire pain a glorious hero. Open your eyes and look. Do you see how the east wars with the wes.? It is love's first conflict—the new bride trembles under the elder's embraces, she struggles and suffers—but soon she shall rejoice, and thousands of torches shall be lighted and radiate peace and gladness, because he shall he born, the young, the strong, the beautiful princeling, who shall rule over all peoples and whose sceptre is called love and whose crown is called light and whose name is the new age! Thorfinn! do you remember the saga about Thor at Utgorda Loake? He lifted the cat so high that the trolls turned pale; he drank so deep from the horn that the trolls trembled—but when the old woman felled him to his knees then the trolls laughed. It was the age that vanquished him, and it is the age that you have warred against, and which has slain you—it is the lord of the age, it is God who has crushed you.

THORFINN. I have never known any god but my own strength, and that god I believe in!

ORM. You don't know him—you who have so long been lying at feud with him. It was he who drove you from your native land, and you thought you were escaping him. It was he who struck your ships to splinters and swallowed up your treasures and ended your power. It was he who tore your child from you—and you said you lacked peace! It was he—[Messenger enters.]

MESSENGER. Are you the Erl Thorfinn.

THORFINN. I am.

MESSENGER. You committed the coast massacre at Reyd-fiord last spring?

THORFINN [Undisturbed]. I did.

MESSENGER. You plundered and burned Hallfred at Thorvalla?

THORFINN. Yes.

MESSENGER. And then you disappeared.

THORFINN [Silent.]

MESSENGER. The Allting has now declared you an outlaw and pronounced you a felon. Your house is to be burned to the ground, and whomsoever will may take your life. Your enemies are at hand, therefore fly while there is yet time—make your escape this night.

[Messenger goes out and there is a long pause.]

ORM. Do you know who that was?

THORFINN. You may well ask that.

ORM. It—was a messenger from that old woman who felled Thor—the age!

THORFINN. You talk like an old woman.

ORM. This age does not want to use force, but you have violated it and it strikes you.

THORFINN. This age cannot suffer strength, therefore it worships weakness.

ORM. When you came to this island you swore peace. You have broken your oath, you have violated your honor, therefore you must die like a felon.

THORFINN. Do you too call me a felon?

ORM. Yes.

THORFINN. Would you dare to break an oath? Would you dare to in called a felon?

ORM [Silent.]

THORFINN. Poor wretch! It is you who put shackles on me when I want to fly! Like a snake you coil yourself around my legs. Let go of me!

ORM. We have sworn the oath of foster-brothers.

THORFINN. I break it!

ORM. You cannot.

THORFINN. Then I'll kick you out of the way.

ORM. That will be our death.

THORFINN. Are you a man, Orm?

ORM. I've become a poet only.

THORFINN. Therefore you have become nothing.

ORM. I knew what I wanted, but I could not attain it. You could attain anything, but did not know what you wanted.

THORFINN. Thanks for your song. Farewell.

ORM. Who will sing your death song?

THORFINN. The ravens no doubt.

ORM. Do you dare to die, Thorfinn?

THORFINN. I dare more! I dare to be forgotten!

ORM. You were always stronger than I. Farewell. We'll meet again. [Orm goes out.]

THORFINN. Alone! Alone! Alone! [Pause.] I remember one autumn when the equinoctial storm raged over England's sun my dragon ship was wrecked and I was tossd up on the rocks alone. Afterward everything grew calm. Oh, what long days and nights! Only the cloudless sky above and endlessly the deep blue sea around me. Not a sound of any living creature! Not even the gulls to wake me with their screeching! Not even a breeze stirred the waves to lap against the stones. It seemed as if I myself were dead! Loudly I talked and shouted, but the sound of my voice frightened me, and thirst bound my tongue. Only the even beat of my heart in my breast told me that I was alive! But after a moment's listening I heard it no longer and, trembling, I rose to my feet, and so it was each time until, senseless, I swooned. When at last I revived I heard the slow beats of a heart beside me and a deep breathing that was not mine, and courage revived in my soul. I looked about—it was a seal seeking rest; it gazed at me with its moist eyes as if filled with compassion for me. Now I was no longer alone! I stretched out my hand to caress its rough body; then it fled and I was doubly alone. Again I am on the rocks! What do I fear? Yes, loneliness! What is loneliness? It is I, myself! Who am I then to fear myself? Am I not Erl Thorfinn, the strong, who has bowed thousands of wills to his? Who never asked for friendship or love but himself bore his own sorrows! No! No! I am another! And therefore Thorfinn the strong fears Thorfinn the weak! Who stole my strength? Who struck me down? Was it the sea? Have I not vanquished the sea three times ten voyages? And it, has defeated me but once—but then to the death! It was the stronger. It was a God. But who subdued the sea that lately raged? Who? Who? Who? It was the stronger! Who are you then, the stronger! Oh, answer, that I may believe! He does not answer!—All is silent!—Again I hear my heart beating. Oh, help, help! I am cold, I freeze—[Goes to door and calls Valgerd.]

[Enter a thrall.]

THRALL. You called, Master Erl?

THORFINN [Recovering himself]. You were mistaken.

THRALL. Yes, master.

THORFINN. How many men are we?

THRALL. Oh—half three score I think.

THORFINN. Are you afraid to die, thrall?

THRALL. How can I be when I believe that I shall be saved?

[Crosses himself.]

THORFINN. What does that mean?

THRALL. The bishop has taught us to do that.

THORFINN. I forgot that you are a Christian.

145

THRALL. Do you wish me to stay in your service when you are a heathen?

THORFINN. I want to prove how little I respect their belief. We must put double bolts on the north gate!

THRALL. Yes, Master, but the belief is stronger than a hundred bolts.

THORFINN. Who questioned you? [Pause.] What happened when you became Christians here on the island?

THRALL. Oh, it was easier than any one would think. They only poured water on us and the bishop read from a big book and then they gave us each a white shirt.

THORFINN. Tell the twelve strongest to take their new axes—do you hear?

THRALL [Starting to go]. Yes, Master.

THORFINN. Wait. [Pause.] Do you remember what was written in that big book?

THRALL. I don't remember much of it, but there was something about two thieves who were hanged on crosses along with the Son of God. But one of them went to heaven.

THORFINN. Did they pour water on him, too?

THRALL. The bishop didn't say.

THORFINN. Do you know whether there are any horses in the stable?

THRALL. They must be out at pasture—but I'll see. [Starts to go.]

THORFINN. You mustn't leave me—Stay. [Pause.] Could you die in peace this night?

THRALL. Yes, if I only had time for a prayer first.

THORFINN. Does that bring peace to one?

THRALL. Oh, yes, Master.

THORFINN [Rises, takes up a goblet]. This you shall have if you will pray for me.

THRALL. That's not enough.

THORFINN. You shall have ten, but if you ever tell of it—I'll take your life.

THRALL. It would not help even if you gave me a hundred. You must pray yourself.

THORFINN. I cannot, but. I command you to pray.

THRALL. I will obey—but you will see that it does not help. [Praying.] Jesus Christ, have pity on this poor sinner who begs for mercy.

THORFINN. That's a lie. I never begged for anything!

THRALL. You see now that it doesn't help.

THORFINN. Give me my armor and help me buckle.

THRALL [Helping]. You are not keeping still. I can't fasten the buckles.

THORFINN. Wretch!

THRALL. But your whole body is shaking.

THORFINN. That's a lie!

[Valgerd and Gunloed enter.]

THRALL. May I go now?

THORFINN. Go.

VALGERD [Coming forward]. You called me.

THORFINN. That's not true.

VALGERD. Your enemies are upon you.

THORFINN. What does that concern you?

VALGRED. Make ready. I have heard what has come to pass.

THORFINN. Then it is best that you [indicating both Valgerd and Gunloed] hide yourselves in the cellar passage.

[Another messenger enters.]

MESSENGER. Erl Thorfinn, we are here. Will you surrender to our superior strength?

THORFINN [Silent.]

MESSENGER. You do not answer. Let the women go as we shall burn your home. [Thorfinn is silent.] Your answer!

[Gunloed who has been standing by the door, comes forward and takes a battle axe from wall.]

GUNLOED. I give you your answer! Ill must Erl Thorfinn have brought up his daughter and little would his wife have loved him if they should desert him now. Here is your answer. [Throws battle axe at messenger's feet.]

MESSENGER. You are stronger than I thought, Thorfinn. For your daughter's sake you shall have a chance to fall like a hero and not as a felon. Make ready for open conflict—out on the field. [Goes out.]

THORFINN [to Valgerd]. Out on you, cowardly, faithless woman, to guard my treasure so ill! To make my child mine enemy.

GUNLOED. O, my father, am I your enemy?

THORFINN. You are a Christian; but it is not too late yet. Will you deny the white Christ?

GUNLOED. Never! But I will follow you to death.

VALGERD. Thorfinn, you call me cowardly. I can suffer that, but faithless—there you wrong me. I have not loved you as warmly as the southern women are said to love, yet have I been faithful to you throughout life and I have sworn to go with you in death—as is the ancient custom. [Opens a trap door in floor.] Look, here have I prepared my grave, here would I die under these smoky beams that have witnessed my sorrows—and with those [points to the carved images of Thor and Odin on uprights of high bench] who guided us here. I want to go with the flames, and in the smoke shall my spirit rise to Ginde to receive charity and peace.

GUNLOED. And I to be alone afterward! Oh, let me follow you.

VALGERD. No, child, you are young. You may yet flourish in a milder clime. But the old fir tree dies on its roots.

GUNLOED. Father, father, you must not die. I will save you!

THORFINN. You?

GUNLOED. Your kinsman Gunnar lies off Hjaerleif's headland with his men. Send one of the thralls to him by a roundabout route and he will come.

THORFINN. So! It wax out of that well that you drew your courage. Keep your help and go if you will.

GUNLOED. You shall not think me a coward. I go with you, mother. You cannot hinder me.

[Thorfinn goes to the door, trying to conceal his emotion.]

VALGERD. No! Stay, Thorfinn, and for once bare your big soul that I may read its dim runics.

THORFINN. If you cannot interpret them now then may this runic stone crumble to air unread.

VALGERD. You are not the hard stone you would seem. You have feelings. Show them. Let them flow forth and you shall know peace!

THORFINN. My feelings are my heart's blood. Would you see it?

[The clatter of arms is heard outside which continues until Thorfinn returns. Thorfinn starts to go out when he hears the chatter.]

VALGERD. Oh, stay and say a word of farewell!

THORFINN. Woman, you tear down my strength with your feelings. Let me go! The play has begun!

VALGERD. Say farewell, at least.

THORNFINN [Restraining his feelings with effort]. Farewell, child. [Goes out.]

VALGERD. That man no one will bend.

GUNLOED. God will!

VALGERD. His hardness is great.

GUNLOED. God's mercy is greater!

VALGERD. Farewell, my child.

GUNLOED. Do you dare leave me behind, alone?

VALGERD [Embracing Gunloed]. Are you prepared?

GUNLOED. The holy virgin prays for me.

VALGERD. I trust in the God of love.

GUNLOED. And in the mother of God.

VALGERD. I know her not.

GUNLOED. You must believe in her.

VALGERD. My belief is not your belief.

GUNLOED [Embracing Valgerd]. Forgive me.

VALGERD. Now to your place.

[Gunloed opens the wooden shutter at window-hole and looks out. Valgerd takes it torch and places herself by the trap door in floor.]

GUNLOED. The strife is sharp.

VALGERD. Do you see the Erl?

GUNLOED. He stands at the gate.

VALGERD. How fares he?

GUNLOED. Everything falls before him.

VALGERD. Does he weary?

GUNLOED. Still is he straight——See what terrible northern lights.

VALGERD. Have many fallen?

GUNLOED. I cannot tell. They are drawing away from the threshing yard. Oh, the heavens are red as blood!

[Pause.]

VALGERD. Speak! What do you see?

GUNLOED [With joy]. The silver falcon!

VALGERD. It's an ill-omen.

GUNLOED. Father comes.

VALGERD. Is he wounded?

GUNLOED. Oh, now he is falling!

VALGERD. Close the window-hole and trust in God.

GUNLOED. No, not yet. A moment.

VALGRED. Are you afraid?

GUNLOED [Going toward door]. No! No!

[The sounds of the conflict gradually die away.]

THORFINN [Comes in pale and wounded.] Stay!

[Valgerd goes towards him. Pause.]

THORFINN [On high bench]. Come here.

[Valgerd and Gunloed go to him. Thorfinn caresses Gunloed's hair, kisses her forehead, then presses Valgerd's hand.]

THORFINN [Kissing Valgerd]. Now you see my heart's blood.

[Valgerd rises to get torch.]

VALGERD. Now is our parting over.

THORFINN. Stay and live with your child.

VALGERD. My oath!

THORFINN. My whole life has been a broken oath and yet I hope——It is better to live——

[Orm comes in wounded. Stops at door.]

ORM. May I come?

THORFINN. Come.

ORM. Have you found peace now?

THORFINN [Caressing the woman]. Soon, soon!

ORM. Then we are ready for the journey.

THORFINN [Looks at Valgerd and Gunloed]. Not yet.

ORM [Sits on bench]. Hurry if you want company.

THORFINN. Orm, are you a Christian?

ORM. You may ask indeed.

THORFINN. What are you then, riddle?

ORM. I was everything. I was nothing. I was a poet.

THORFINN. Do you believe in anything?

ORM. I've come to have a belief.

THORFINN. What gave it to you?

ORM. Doubt, misfortune, sorrow.

THORFINN [To Valgerd]. Valgerd, give me your hand, so. Hold fast—tighter—you must not let go until—the end.

[Gunnar comes in and stops by door.]

THORFINN. Who comes?

GUNNAR. You know me!

THORFINN. I know your voice, but my eyes see you not.

GUNNAR. I am your kinsman, Gunnar.

THORFINN [After a pause]. Step forth.

[Gunnar remains where he is, looking questioningly at Gunloed.]

THORFINN. Is he here?

[Gunloed rises, goes with slow steps and bowed head to Gunnar. Takes his hand and leads him to Thorfinn. They kneel.]

THORFINN [Putting hands on their heads]. Eternal—— Creating——God—[Dies.]

CURTAIN.

THE STRONGER

CHARACTERS
> MME. X., an actress, married
> MLLE. Y., an actress, unmarried
> A WAITRESS

[SCENE—The corner of a ladies' cafe. Two little iron tables, a red velvet sofa, several chairs. Enter Mme. X., dressed in winter clothes, carrying a Japanese basket on her arm.]

[MLLE. Y. sits with a half empty beer bottle before her, reading an illustrated paper, which she changes later for another.]

MME. X. Good afternoon, Amelie. You're sitting here alone on Christmas eve like a poor bachelor!

MLLE. Y. [Looks up, nods, and resumes her reading.]

MME. X. Do you know it really hurts me to see you like this, alone, in a cafe, and on Christmas eve, too. It makes me feel as I did one time when I saw a bridal party in a Paris restaurant, and the bride sat reading a comic paper, while the groom played billiards with the witnesses. Huh, thought I, with such a beginning, what will follow, and what will be the end? He played billiards on his wedding eve! [Mlle. Y. starts to speak]. And she read a comic paper, you mean? Well, they are not altogether the same thing.

[A waitress enters, places a cup of chocolate before Mme. X. and goes out.]

MME. X. You know what, Amelie! I believe you would have done better to have kept him! Do you remember, I was the first to say "Forgive him?" Do you remember that? You would be married now and have a home. Remember that Christmas when you went out to visit your fiance's parents in the country? How you gloried in the happiness of home life and really longed to quit the theatre forever? Yes, Amelie dear, home is the best of all, the theatre next and children—well, you don't understand that.

MLLE. Y. [Looks up scornfully.]

[Mme. X. sips a few spoonfuls out of the cup, then opens her basket and shows Christmas presents.]

MME. X. Now you shall see what I bought for my piggywigs. [Takes up a doll.] Look at this! This is for Lisa, ha! Do you see how she can roll her eyes and turn her head, eh? And here is Maja's popgun. [Loads it and shoots at Mlle. Y.]

MLLE. Y. [Makes a startled gesture.]

MME. X. Did I frighten you? Do you think I would like to shoot you, eh? On my soul, if I don't think you did! If you wanted to shoot *me* it wouldn't be so surprising, because I stood in your way—and I know you can never forget that—although I was absolutely innocent. You still believe I intrigued and got you out of the Stora theatre, but I didn't. I didn't do that, although you think so. Well, it doesn't make any difference what I say to you. You still believe I did it. [Takes up a pair of embroidered slippers.] And these are for my better half. I embroidered them myself—I can't bear tulips, but he wants tulips on everything.

MLLE. Y. [Looks up ironically and curiously.]

MME. X. [Putting a hand in each slipper.] What little feet Bob has! What? And you should see what a splendid stride he has! You've never seen him in slippers! [Mlle. Y. laughs aloud.] Look! [She makes the slippers walk on the table. Mlle. Y. laughs loudly.] And when he is grumpy he stamps like this with his foot. "What! damn those servants who can never learn to make coffee. Oh, now those creatures haven't trimmed the lamp wick properly!" And then there are draughts on the floor and his feet are cold. "Ugh, how cold it is; the stupid idiots can never keep the fire going." [She rubs the slippers together, one sole over the other.]

MLLE. Y. [Shrieks with laughter.]

MME. X. And then he comes home and has to hunt for his slippers which Marie has stuck under the chiffonier—oh, but it's sinful to sit here and make fun of one's husband this way when he is kind and a good little man. You ought to have had such a husband, Amelie. What are you laughing at? What? What? And you see he's true to me. Yes, I'm sure of that, because he told me himself—what are you laughing at?—that when I was touring in Norway that that brazen Frederique came and wanted to seduce him! Can you fancy anything so infamous? [Pause.] I'd have torn her eyes out if she had come to see him when I was at home. [Pause.] It was lucky that Bob told me about it himself and that it didn't reach me through gossip. [Pause.] But would you believe it, Frederique wasn't the only one! I don't know why, but the women are crazy about my husband. They must think he has influence about getting them theatrical engagements, because he is connected with the government. Perhaps you were after him yourself. I didn't use to trust you any too much. But now I know he never bothered his head about you, and you always seemed to have a grudge against him someway.

[Pause. They look at each other in a puzzled way.]

MME. X. Come and see us this evening, Amelie, and show us that you're not put out with us,—not put out with me at any rate. I don't know, but I think it would be uncomfortable to have you for an enemy. Perhaps it's because I stood in your way [rallentando] or—I really—don't know why—in particular.

[Pause. Mlle. Y. stares at Mme. X curiously.]

MME. X [Thoughtfully]. Our acquaintance has been so queer. When I saw you for the first time I was afraid of you, so afraid that I didn't dare let you out of my sight; no matter when or where, I always found myself near you—I didn't dare have you for an enemy, so I became your friend. But there was always discord when you came to our house, because I saw that my husband couldn't endure you, and the whole thing seemed as awry to me as an ill-fitting gown—and I did all I could to make him friendly toward you, but with no success until you became engaged. Then came a violent friendship between you, so that it looked all at once as though you both dared show your real feelings only when you were secure— and then—how was it later? I didn't get jealous—strange to say! And I remember at the christening, when you acted as godmother, I made him kiss you—he did so, and you became so confused—as it were; I didn't notice it then—didn't think about it later, either— have never thought about it until—now! [Rises suddenly.] Why are you silent? You haven't said a word this whole time, but you have let me go on talking! You have sat there, and your eyes have reeled out of me all these thoughts which lay like raw silk in its cocoon— thoughts—suspicious thoughts, perhaps. Let me see—why did you break your engagement? Why do you never come to our house any more? Why won't you come to see us tonight?

[Mlle. Y. appears as if about to speak.]

MME. X. Hush, you needn't speak—I understand it all! It was because—and because—and because! Yes, yes! Now all the accounts balance. That's it. Fie, I won't sit at the same table with you. [Moves her things to another table.] That's the reason I had to embroider tulips—which I hate—on his slippers, because you are fond of tulips; that's why [Throws slippers on the floor] we go to Lake Maelarn in the summer, because you don't like salt water; that's why my boy is named Eskil—because it's your father's name; that's why I wear your colors, read your authors, eat your favorite dishes, drink your drinks—chocolate, for instance; that's why—oh—my God—it's terrible, when I think about it; it's terrible. Everything, everything came from you to me, even your passions. Your soul crept into mine, like a worm into an apple, ate and ate, bored and bored, until nothing was left but the rind and a little black dust within. I wanted to get away from you, but I couldn't; you lay like a snake and charmed me with your black eyes; I felt that when I lifted my wings they only dragged me down; I lay in the water with bound feet, and the stronger I strove to keep up the deeper I worked myself down, down, until I sank to the bottom, where you lay like a giant crab to clutch me in your claws—and there I am lying now.

I hate you, hate you, hate you! And you only sit there silent—silent and indifferent; indifferent whether it's new moon or waning moon, Christmas or New Year's, whether others are happy or unhappy; without power to hate or to love; as quiet as a stork by a rat hole— you couldn't scent your prey and capture it, but you could lie in wait for it! You sit here in your corner of the cafe—did you know it's called "The Rat Trap" for you?—and read the papers to see if misfortune hasn't befallen some one, to see if some one hasn't been given notice at the theatre, perhaps; you sit here and calculate about your next victim and reckon on your chances of recompense like a pilot in a shipwreck. Poor Amelie, I pity you, nevertheless, because I know you are unhappy, unhappy like one who has been wounded, and angry because you are wounded. I can't be angry with you, no matter how much I want to be—because you come out the weaker one. Yes, all that with Bob doesn't trouble me. What is that to me, after all? And what difference does it make whether I learned to drink chocolate from you or some one else. [Sips a spoonful from her cup.]

Besides, chocolate is very healthful. And if you taught me how to dress—tant mieux!—that has only made me more attractive to my husband; so you lost and I won there. Well, judging by certain signs, I believe you have already lost him; and you certainly intended that I should leave him—do as you did with your fiance and regret as you now regret; but, you see, I don't do that—we mustn't be too exacting. And why should I take only what no one else wants?

Perhaps, take it all in all, I am at this moment the stronger one. You received nothing from me, but you gave me much. And now I seem like a thief since you have awakened and find I possess what is your loss. How could it be otherwise when everything is worthless and sterile in your hands? You can never keep a man's love with your tulips and your passions—but I can keep it. You can't learn how to live from your authors, as I have learned. You have no little Eskil to cherish, even if your father's name was Eskil. And why are you always silent, silent, silent? I thought that was strength, but perhaps it is because you have nothing to say! Because you never think about anything! [Rises and picks up slippers.]

Now I'm going home—and take the tulips with me—*your* tulips! You are unable to learn from another; you can't bend—therefore, you broke like a dry stalk. But I won't break! Thank you, Amelie, for all your good lessons. Thanks for teaching my husband how to love. Now I'm going home to love him. [Goes.]

BIBLIOBAZAAR

The essential book market!

Did you know that you can get any of our titles in large print?

Did you know that we have an ever-growing collection of books in many languages?

Order online:
www.bibliobazaar.com

Find all of your favorite classic books!

Stay up to date with the latest government reports!

At BiblioBazaar, we aim to make knowledge more accessible by making thousands of titles available to you- *quickly and affordably*.

Contact us:
BiblioBazaar
PO Box 21206
Charleston, SC 29413